MEALS from the Mediterranean

Set sail on a voyage of discovery to the lands lapped by the Mediterranean, countries whose cuisines have certain characteristics in common, including an abundance of fish and ample use of colourful vegetables like tomatoes and aubergines, but which retain those individual attributes that gives each of them a culinary style that is wholly unique.

From Spain comes paella and a chicken casserole with tomatoes and pimientos; the South of France contributes bouillabaisse, the famous salad niçoise and a winter warmer in the form of a hearty daube de boeuf.

Italy is perhaps best known for pasta, but also has marvellous meat dishes. Veal is the preferred meat, but chicken breasts, pork fillet or thin pork steaks can often be used instead. From Italy, too, comes risotto and egg dishes like the famous frittata.

Cross to Greece and linger over a variety of tasty appetizers (meze) before sampling tender lamb in casseroles or on kebabs. Filo pastry is a speciality of this part of the Mediterranean – try it in borek, in spinach and cheese pie, or with a rich nut filling in baklava.

Many other countries have contributed to the melting pot that may loosely be termed Mediterranean food. Some of the best loved recipes are to be found in this collection. Try them at home (menu suggestions are on pages 44-46) and discover that you don't have to travel to give your taste buds a treat!

CONTENTS

SOUPS AND STARTERS	2
FISH AND SHELLFISH	9
EGGS AND CHEESE	17
PASTA, RICE AND POLENTA	20
MEAT AND POULTRY	24
VEGETABLES AND SALADS	32
DESSERTS	38
MEDITERRANEAN FOOD ON THE MENU	44
INDEX	48

Soups and Starters

It would be easy to devote an entire book to the soups and starters of the Mediterranean, from the delicately-flavoured Avgolemono to the robust and richly-coloured Bouillabaisse. Starters or appetizers have become a unique culinary experience in countries like Greece, Turkey and the Lebanon, where there may be as many as fifty meze – or hors d'oevres – on the menu.

Yogurt Soup

1.5 litres (2½pt) chicken stock
60g (2oz) long grain rice
600ml (1pt) natural low fat yogurt
3 egg yolks
30g (1oz) butter, melted
2 tblspn chopped fresh mint

1 Bring the chicken stock to the boil in a large saucepan. Add the rice and cook for 15 minutes or until tender.

2 In a second (larger) saucepan, beat the yogurt and egg yolks together until well mixed.

3 Slowly pour the hot stock and rice mixture into the pan containing the yogurt and egg yolks. Heat gently, stirring constantly until the soup thickens.

4 Ladle the soup into serving bowls. Spoon a little melted butter onto each portion and sprinkle with mint. Serve at once.

Serves 4

Avgolemono

Illustrated on page 46

1.5 litres (2½pt) chicken stock
90g (3oz) long grain rice
4 egg yolks
60ml (2fl oz) lemon juice
salt
freshly ground black pepper
1 tblspn chopped fresh parsley

1 Bring the chicken stock to the boil in a large saucepan. Add the rice and cook for 15 minutes or until tender.

2 In a bowl, beat the egg yolks until pale and creamy, using a hand-held electric mixer. Add the lemon juice and mix well.

3 Strain the rice, reserving the stock. Set aside 185ml (6fl oz) of the stock in a jug; pour the rest back into the clean pan and simmer until required. Reserve the rice.

4 Slowly pour 60ml (2fl oz) of the measured stock into the lemon and egg mixture, stirring well.

5 Stir in a further 125ml (4fl oz) of stock, then slowly pour the egg mixture into the pan of simmering stock, stirring constantly until the soup thickens.

6 Add the reserved rice to the soup, season with salt and pepper, garnish with parsley and serve at once.

Serves 6

Yogurt Soup

Bouillabaisse

Illustrated on pages 44/45

60ml (2fl oz) olive oil
2 onions, sliced
1 large stick celery, chopped
2 cloves garlic, crushed
1 large carrot, sliced
1 bay leaf
185ml (6fl oz) dry white wine
2 x 410g (13oz) cans chopped tomatoes
250ml (8fl oz) chicken stock
2 x 60g (2oz) cans tomato purée
250g (8oz) calamari rings
500g (1lb) mussels, scrubbed and bearded
250g (8oz) peeled cooked prawns
1 cooked lobster, flesh chopped, tail shell reserved
2 tblspn chopped fresh parsley

1 Heat the oil in a large saucepan over moderate heat. Add the onions, celery, garlic, carrot and bay leaf. Cook, stirring constantly, for 5 minutes.

2 Add the wine and cook until reduced by half. Stir in the tomatoes, stock and tomato purée. Simmer for 15 minutes.

3 Stir in the calamari and mussels. Simmer for 5 minutes until the mussel shells open. Discard any that remain closed.

4 Add the cooked prawns and lobster and heat through for 1 minute. Remove the bay leaf, sprinkle the soup with the chopped parsley and garnish with the lobster tail shell. Serve at once.
Serves 4

Kitchen Tip
One of the classic accompaniments for bouillabaisse is rouille: Whisk 2 egg yolks, 2 crushed cloves garlic, 1 tspn caster sugar and a little salt and pepper together, then slowly whisk in 250ml (8fl oz) olive oil, adding it drop by drop at first, until the mixture is thick and creamy.

Hearty Bean and Vegetable Soup

Hearty Bean and Vegetable Soup

185g (6oz) haricot beans, soaked overnight in water to cover
1 tblspn oil
2 onions, chopped
2 cloves garlic, crushed
2 carrots, sliced
2 sticks celery, sliced
2 potatoes, chopped
1 x 410g (13oz) can chopped tomatoes
1.5 litres (2½pt) water
2 tblspn chopped parsley for garnish

1 Drain beans. Bring a large saucepan of water to boil, add beans and boil vigorously for 10 minutes, then simmer for 30-40 minutes more until tender. Drain, reserving 500ml (16fl oz) of cooking liquid. Purée half the beans with reserved cooking liquid. Set aside with remaining beans.

2 Heat the oil in a saucepan, add onions and garlic and fry until tender. Add carrots, celery, potatoes, tomatoes with can juices, measured water, beans and bean purée. Bring to boil, then simmer, covered, for 20 minutes or until vegetables are tender. Stir in the parsley and serve.
Serves 4

Taramasalata

2 slices white bread, crusts removed
60ml (2fl oz) cold water
155g (5oz) smoked cod's roe, skinned and quartered
1 clove garlic
juice of 1 lemon
150ml (5fl oz) olive oil
freshly ground black pepper
2 tblspn very finely chopped onion
pitta wedges to serve

1 Soak bread in measured water for 5 minutes. Squeeze dry; transfer to a food processor or blender. Add roe with the garlic and lemon juice and purée until smooth.

2 With machine running, add olive oil, at first drop by drop, then in a steady stream, until mixture has consistency of mayonnaise. Add black pepper to taste.

3 Add onion; process to blend. Spoon taramasalata into a bowl, cover and refrigerate for at least 2 hours. Serve with pitta wedges.
Makes about 250ml (8fl oz)

Tzatziki

1 large cucumber
500ml (16fl oz) Greek yogurt or natural low fat yogurt
1 tblspn finely chopped fresh mint
1 tblspn chopped fresh parsley
2 cloves garlic, crushed
pitta bread or sliced French bread to serve

Peel cucumber and grate roughly. Stir in yogurt, mint, parsley and garlic. Cover, refrigerate for at least 1 hour. Serve with sliced bread for dipping.
Serves 8

Tzatziki

Dolmades

40 drained vine leaves in brine
315g (10oz) minced lamb
90g (3oz) cooked long grain rice
1 onion, very finely chopped
1 tspn dried thyme
2 tblspn chopped fresh parsley
2 tblspn lemon juice

1 Rinse vine leaves under hot water to remove salt. Pat dry.

2 Combine lamb, rice, onion, thyme and parsley.

3 Place a vine leaf vein side up on work surface. Place 1 tblspn mince mixture on leaf, near base of stem. Roll up leaf into a sausage shape, tucking in edges to make a neat package. Repeat to use all leaves and filling.

4 Arrange filled vine leaves on base of a large saucepan, packing them in tightly. Cover dolmades with an inverted plate to keep them in place. Pour over lemon juice and add water to cover plate. Simmer rolls for 1 hour, topping up water as necessary. Using a slotted spoon, transfer dolmades to a serving dish. Serve chilled or at room temperature.
Makes 40

Greek Garlic Dip

375g (12oz) mashed potatoes
1 tblspn crushed garlic
90ml (3fl oz) olive oil
1 tblspn lemon juice
1 tblspn vinegar
salt
freshly ground black pepper

1 Combine mashed potatoes and garlic in a large bowl.

2 Stir olive oil, lemon juice and vinegar together. Add to potatoes. Using a hand-held electric mixer, whip mixture until smooth and fluffy. Season. Cover and chill for at least 2 hours. Serve as a dip.
Makes about 500ml (16fl oz)

Cherry Tomatoes with Parmesan and Rosemary

250g (8oz) cherry tomatoes, halved and seeded

freshly ground black pepper

60g (2oz) grated Parmesan cheese

1 tblspn single cream

pinch nutmeg

2 tspn fresh rosemary, finely chopped

1 Preheat grill. Sprinkle the inside of the tomatoes with black pepper.

2 In a small bowl, combine the cheese, cream, nutmeg and rosemary. Mix well.

3 Spoon the mixture into the tomatoes and grill for 2-3 minutes. Serve immediately.
Serves 4

Italian Bean Salad

250g (8oz) drained canned butterbeans

250g (8oz) drained canned red kidney beans

125g (4oz) button mushrooms, sliced

2 tblspn snipped chives

60ml (2fl oz) lemon juice

60ml (2fl oz) olive oil

1 clove garlic, crushed

2 tblspn dried basil

60g (2oz) thinly sliced salami

1 Mix the beans, mushrooms and chives in a large bowl. Whisk together lemon juice, oil, garlic and basil. Pour over bean mixture, toss well. Marinate for 1 hour.

2 Cut salami slices in half and arrange around rim of a salad bowl. Fill centre with bean salad. Serve.
Serves 4

Grilled Aubergine with Mozzarella

3 tblspn olive oil

1 garlic clove, crushed

1/4 tspn freshly ground black pepper

1 medium aubergine, cut into 8 x 1cm (1/2in) slices

8 thin slices mozzarella cheese

2 drained canned pimientos, sliced into strips

1 Preheat grill. Combine oil, garlic and pepper. Brush mixture over aubergine slices.

2 Grill aubergine slices for 3 minutes on each side until lightly browned.

3 Top each slice with mozzarella; decorate with a lattice of pimiento strips and grill until cheese melts. Serve immediately.
Makes 8

Crudités with Aubergine and Olive Purée

1 large aubergine

2 cloves garlic, unpeeled

90g (3oz) pitted black olives

2-3 tspn olive oil

salt and freshly ground black pepper

a mixture of raw vegetables for dipping, eg. carrot and courgette sticks, cauliflower florets, red and green pepper sticks, whole blanched green beans

1 Preheat oven to 200°C (400°F/Gas 6). Bake aubergine whole for 40 minutes or until soft. Cut in half lengthwise; allow to cool.

2 Cook whole garlic cloves in boiling water for 15 minutes; drain and peel.

3 Scoop aubergine pulp into a food processor or blender, add garlic and olives, with 2 tspn of oil. Purée until smooth, adding more oil if necessary. Season. Serve with raw vegetables for dipping.
Makes about 500ml (16fl oz)

Cherry Tomatoes with Parmesan and Rosemary, Grilled Aubergine with Mozzarella

Hummus

Borek

250g (8oz) feta cheese

90g (3oz) grated Parmesan cheese

2 eggs, beaten

4 tblspn chopped fresh parsley

salt

freshly ground black pepper

375g (12oz) filo pastry, thawed if frozen

125ml (4fl oz) butter, melted

1 Preheat oven to 180°C (350°F/Gas 4). Crumble feta and mash with a fork. Stir in Parmesan, eggs and parsley, season to taste.

2 Cut filo lengthwise into 5cm (2in) wide strips. Remove one strip, keeping the rest covered with a damp tea towel. Brush the strip with melted butter.

3 Place 1 tspn of filling at end of strip and fold over corner to make a triangle. Continue folding strip from side to side, keeping triangle shape, until all the pastry has been used. Repeat with remaining strips.

4 Arrange borek on lightly greased baking sheets, brush with remaining butter and bake for 15 minutes until crisp

Makes about 50

Hummus

220g (7oz) chickpeas, soaked for 4 hours in water to cover

125ml (4fl oz) tahini (sesame seed paste)

½ tspn salt

¼ tspn freshly ground black pepper

60ml (2fl oz) lemon juice

3 cloves garlic, crushed

90g (3oz) ricotta cheese

paprika

3 tblspn olive oil

1 Drain chickpeas and place in a large saucepan. Cover with fresh water, bring to the boil, simmer for 1-1¼ hours or until tender. Drain, reserving 250ml (8fl oz) of cooking water.

2 Purée chickpeas with the reserved cooking water, tahini, salt, pepper, lemon juice, garlic and ricotta until smooth.

3 Spoon hummus onto a shallow plate, sprinkle with paprika and drizzle with olive oil. Serve with pitta bread.

Serves 6

Tomato and Bocconcini Salad

12 leaves curly endive

6 ripe tomatoes, thinly sliced

6 bocconcini, thinly sliced or 125g (4oz) sliced mozzarella

60ml (2fl oz) olive oil

salt

freshly ground black pepper

2 tblspn roughly chopped fresh basil

Spread endive leaves on a platter. Arrange tomato and cheese slices alternately in concentric circles on top of endive, drizzle with oil. Season. Scatter with basil.

Serves 8-12

FISH AND SHELLFISH

Lands bounded by the Mediterranean share a common bounty: the sea's rich harvest. From simple steamed shellfish to richly flavoured stews, famous dishes like Paella, Moules au Gratin and Sardinian Fish Stew have made a valuable contribution to International cuisine.

Crab Sauté with Prosciutto

30g (1oz) butter

250g (8oz) freshly cooked crabmeat

2 spring onions, finely chopped

1 tblspn chopped fresh parsley

1/4 tspn freshly ground black pepper

1 tblspn lemon juice

1/4 tspn chilli paste or 1 tspn chopped fresh chilli

8 slices prosciutto

lemon twist and parsley sprig for garnish

1 Melt the butter in a medium saucepan over moderate heat. Stir in the crab, spring onions, parsley, pepper, lemon juice and chilli paste or fresh chilli. Cook for 1 minute.

2 Arrange 2 slices of prosciutto on each plate, then divide the crab mixture between them. Garnish with lemon and parsley and serve at once.
Serves 4

Kitchen Tip
The easiest way to chop the parsley is to place it in a mug and snip it with kitchen scissors.

Crab Sauté with Prosciutto

Mussels in Garlic and Basil Tomato Sauce

2.25kg (5lb) mussels

75g (2 1/2 oz) salt

250ml (8fl oz) water

5 tblspn olive oil

2 cloves garlic

6 fresh basil leaves

4 ripe tomatoes, peeled, finely chopped

freshly ground black pepper

1 Place mussels in a sink of cold water. Add salt, mix well. Soak for 1 hour.

2 Drain mussels, scrub with a stiff brush under cold running water and pull away beards. Discard any open mussels, or any that remain open when tapped.

3 Place mussels in a large saucepan with measured water. Add 2 tablespoons oil. Steam mussels in batches in covered pan until they open, shaking pan constantly. Discard any mussels that remain shut. Shell mussels, reserving a few shells for garnish. Strain pan juices and set aside.

4 Place garlic and basil in a mortar and grind to a paste with a pestle. Heat remaining oil in a frying pan, add garlic paste and cook over low heat for 1 minute. Add tomatoes, with pepper to taste.

5 Add about 125ml (4fl oz) of the reserved pan juices. Simmer for 5 minutes until the sauce starts to thicken. Return mussels to pan and heat gently for about 8 minutes. Serve hot, garnished with mussel shells.
Serves 4

Fried Halibut Steaks with Oregano

4 halibut steaks

salt

freshly ground black pepper

30g (1oz) flour

60ml (2fl oz) olive oil

60ml (2fl oz) vegetable oil

2 tspn chopped fresh oregano

2 tblspn lemon juice

lemon wedges for serving

1 Sprinkle the halibut steaks with salt and freshly ground black pepper. Spread out the flour in a shallow bowl, and roll the fish until lightly coated.

2 Heat the oils in a large frying pan, add the fish and fry for about 5 minutes on each side until golden brown and cooked through.

3 Using a fish slice, transfer the fish to a heated platter. Dust with oregano and sprinkle with lemon juice. Serve garnished with the lemon wedges.

Serves 4

Kitchen Tip

It is important that the oil is hot, but not smoking, before the fish is added.

The fish is cooked when it flakes easily when tested with the tip of a sharp knife.

Moules au Gratin

24 mussels, scrubbed and bearded

250ml (8fl oz) water

1 tblspn chopped fresh basil

90g (3oz) grated Parmesan cheese

60g (2oz) butter, melted

50g (2oz) day-old breadcrumbs

2 cloves garlic, crushed

1 Combine mussels and water in a saucepan and steam mussels over moderate heat for about 3 minutes until they open. Discard any that remain shut.

2 Preheat grill. Remove mussels from pan, discard top shells. Loosen mussel meat in bottom shells.

3 Combine remaining ingredients. Top each mussel with about 1 tablespoon of mixture. Grill until toppings are golden.

Serves 4

Pickled Octopus Salad

12 baby octopus, cleaned

350ml (12fl oz) white wine vinegar

60g (2oz) sugar

3 small cucumbers, sliced

1 tspn yellow mustard seeds

2 tblspn chopped fresh dill

1 Combine octopus, vinegar and sugar in a medium saucepan over moderate heat. Bring to the boil, add cucumber and cook for 2 minutes. Using a slotted spoon, transfer octopus and cucumber to a bowl; cool.

2 Reheat vinegar mixture until boiling, lower heat and simmer for 5 minutes. Cool to room temperature, add to octopus and cucumber mixture and stir. Add mustard seeds and dill, cover and chill until ready.

3 Arrange octopus and cucumber on a serving plate, pour a little vinegar marinade over and serve.

Serves 6

Pickled Octopus Salad

Paella

60ml (2fl oz) olive oil
2 cloves garlic, crushed
1 onion, chopped
3 tomatoes, chopped
1 red pepper, chopped
500g (1lb) cooked chicken, cut into bite-sized portions
1 tspn paprika
¼ tspn powdered saffron
185g (6oz) long grain rice
750ml (1¼pt) chicken stock
125g (4oz) peas, thawed if frozen
250g (8oz) peeled cooked prawns or shrimp

1 Heat oil in a large deep frying pan, add garlic, onion, tomatoes and red pepper. Cook, stirring frequently over moderate heat for 5 minutes. Add chicken, with paprika and saffron.

2 Level mixture in pan, spread rice evenly on top and cook for 3 minutes. Pour stock into mixture and stir.

3 Bring to the boil and cook for 10 minutes. Add peas and prawns and continue to cook until most of the liquid has been absorbed and rice is tender. Serve hot.
Serves 4

Paella

Tuna Steaks with Yogurt Cucumber Sauce

125ml (4fl oz) natural low fat yogurt
3 tblspn mayonnaise
1 tblspn freshly squeezed lime juice
30g (1oz) cucumber, grated
125g (4oz) green seedless grapes
30g (1oz) butter, melted
60ml (2fl oz) lemon juice
4 x 185g (6oz) tuna steaks

1 Preheat grill. Combine yogurt, mayonnaise, lime juice, cucumber and grapes; set aside.

2 Mix butter and lemon juice together; brush tuna steaks with mixture and grill for 4 minutes on each side until cooked.

3 Transfer tuna to serving plates. Serve with yogurt cucumber sauce.
Serves 4

Fish Fillets with Prosciutto and Sun-dried Tomato Topping

2 tblspn olive oil
60g (2oz) thinly sliced prosciutto, cut into strips
4 white fish fillets
2 spring onions, finely chopped
1 x 170g (5½oz) jar sun-dried tomatoes in oil, drained and chopped

1 Heat oil in a large frying pan, add prosciutto and stir until heated. Using a slotted spoon, transfer prosciutto to a small bowl; set aside.

2 Add fish to oil remaining in pan and cook for 2 minutes on each side until opaque.

3 Using a fish slice, transfer the fish to a heated platter, cover with foil and keep hot.

4 Add spring onions to frying pan and cook over moderate heat for 2 minutes. Stir in prosciutto and tomatoes and cook for 3 minutes more. Spoon the sauce over fish. Serve.
Serves 4

Warm Mullet Niçoise

4 whole red mullet, cleaned and heads removed

60ml (2fl oz) olive oil

3 tomatoes, cut into small cubes

1 onion, chopped

2 cloves garlic, crushed

10 pitted black olives, chopped

2 tblspn chopped fresh parsley

250ml (8fl oz) white wine

1 Preheat oven to 180°C (350°F/Gas 4). Place fish in a single layer on a greased shallow baking dish. Brush each fish generously with olive oil and wrap foil around the tails.

2 Combine tomatoes, onion, garlic, olives and parsley and place on and around fish.

3 Pour wine over and bake for 20-25 minutes until fish is cooked. Serve each fish with a portion of tomato mixture.
Serves 4

Calamari with Tomato Mint Sauce

3 tblspn olive oil

2 tblspn crushed garlic

1/2 tspn crushed black peppercorns

1/4 tspn chilli paste

185g (6oz) drained canned chopped tomatoes, puréed

60ml (2fl oz) dry white wine

1 tblspn tomato purée

315g (10oz) small calamari (squid) rings

1 tblspn chopped fresh mint

1 Heat oil in a large saucepan. Add garlic, pepper, chilli paste, puréed tomatoes and wine and cook for 3 minutes.

2 Stir in tomato purée and calamari and cook, stirring, for 2 minutes. Stir in mint.
Serves 4

Fillet of Fish with Mustard Sauce

60g (2oz) butter

4 courgettes, cut into thin strips

2 red peppers, cut into thin strips

2 sticks celery, cut into thin strips

8 white fish fillets

350ml (12fl oz) single cream

1 tblspn wholegrain mustard

1 Melt butter in a large frying pan. Add courgettes, red peppers and celery and sauté for 2 minutes. Transfer vegetables to a baking dish, cover and keep hot.

2 Add fish fillets to butter remaining in pan and fry for 2 minutes on each side until cooked through. Transfer to a platter, cover and keep hot.

3 Add cream to pan, bring to the boil and cook until reduced to about 185ml (6fl oz). Stir in mustard.

4 Divide vegetables between serving plates, place two fish fillets on each, top with mustard sauce.
Serves 4

Prawns with Feta

1 small onion, finely chopped

15g (1/2oz) butter

1 tblspn olive oil

125ml (4fl oz) dry white wine

4 tomatoes, peeled, seeded and chopped

1 clove garlic, crushed

3/4 tspn chopped fresh oregano

salt

freshly ground black pepper

125g (4oz) feta cheese, crumbled

1kg (2lb) uncooked prawns, peeled and deveined

4 tblspn chopped fresh parsley

1 Sauté onion in butter and olive oil in a saucepan for 5 minutes. Add wine, tomatoes, garlic and oregano. Season.

2 Bring to the boil, then simmer until sauce thickens slightly. Add cheese, mix well, then simmer for 10 minutes stirring occasionally.

3 Add prawns and cook over moderate heat for 5 minutes or until tender. Do not overcook. Transfer to a serving dish, sprinkle with parsley.
Serves 4

Bourride

60g (2oz) butter

2 onions, sliced

2 parsnips, sliced

1 litre (1 3/4pt) chicken or fish stock

250ml (8fl oz) white wine

60ml (2fl oz) freshly squeezed lime juice

1 tspn crushed black peppercorns

410g (13oz) sea bream fillet, cut into large chunks

410g (13oz) mussels, scrubbed and bearded

60ml (2fl oz) soured cream

1 1/2 tblspn chopped fresh dill

1 Heat the butter in a large saucepan over moderate heat. Add the onions and parsnips and cook for 2 minutes, stirring constantly.

2 Add the stock, wine, lime juice, pepper, fish and mussels and bring the mixture to just below boiling point. Cover, lower the heat and simmer until the mussel shells open. Discard any mussels that remain shut.

3 Using a slotted spoon, remove the mussels, fish and vegetables. Shell the mussels. Add the soured cream to the stock mixture remaining in the pan; simmer until reduced by half and beginning to thicken.

4 Add the mussels, fish and vegetables to the sauce. Stir in the dill and heat through gently. Serve at once.
Serves 4

Bourride, Calamari with Tomato Mint Sauce

Wine Steamed Mussels with Orange Segments

2 tblspn oil
1 onion, chopped
3 cloves garlic, crushed
2 tblspn chopped fresh oregano
10 strips of orange rind
350ml (12fl oz) dry white wine
750g (1½lb) mussels, scrubbed and bearded
1 tblspn chopped fresh parsley
1 orange, peeled and segmented

1 Heat the oil in a large saucepan over moderate heat. Add the onion and garlic and cook for 2 minutes. Stir in the oregano, orange strips and wine and cook for 2 minutes more.

2 Bring to the boil, add the mussels and cover the pan. Steam the mussels, shaking the pan frequently, until they open. Discard any that remain shut. Using a slotted spoon, transfer the mussels to a serving dish.

3 Stir the parsley into the mussel cooking liquid and bring to the boil. Stir in orange segments. Pour the sauce over the mussels and serve at once.
Serves 2-3

Scallops with Parsley and Wine Sauce

500g (1lb) shelled scallops, deveined
2 cloves garlic, crushed
1 tblspn chopped fresh oregano
90ml (3fl oz) olive oil
300ml (10fl oz) dry white wine
30g (1oz) dried breadcrumbs

1 Combine the scallops, garlic, oregano and 60ml (2fl oz) of the olive oil in a large bowl. Cover and refrigerate for 1 hour.

2 Heat the remaining olive oil in a medium frying pan, add the scallops with the marinade and cook over high heat for 2 minutes.

3 Add the wine and breadcrumbs and stir rapidly for 1 minute.

4 Serve at once, garnished with lemon slices, chopped fresh parsley and a parsley sprig, if liked.
Serves 4

Seafood Salad

185ml (6fl oz) dry white wine
60ml (2fl oz) lemon juice
2 tspn finely chopped chilli
250g (8oz) shelled scallops, deveined
250g (8oz) squid, rinsed and cut into rings
250ml (8fl oz) water
500g (1lb) mussels, scrubbed and bearded
500g (1lb) cooked shelled prawns, tails intact
60ml (2fl oz) olive oil
3 tblspn freshly squeezed lime juice
1 tblspn chopped fresh basil

1 Combine the wine and lemon juice in a large saucepan. Bring to the boil, add the chilli, scallops and squid rings and cook for 2 minutes. Using a slotted spoon, transfer the scallops and squid to a bowl. Set aside.

2 Add the measured water to the liquid remaining in the pan. Bring to the boil, add the mussels, cover and steam until the shells have opened. Discard any that remain shut. Using a slotted spoon, remove mussels and leave to cool.

3 Shell mussels; add meat to scallops and squid. Bring the liquid remaining in the saucepan to the boil, then simmer until reduced to about 125ml (4fl oz). Cool.

4 Stir the prawns into the seafood mixture in the bowl. Mix the reduced pan liquid with the olive oil, lime juice and basil. Pour over the salad, toss lightly, cover and marinate in the refrigerator for 4 hours before serving.
Serves 6

Scallops with Parsley and Wine Sauce, Seafood Salad

Sardinian Fish Stew

2 onions, sliced
2 green peppers, sliced
3 cloves garlic, crushed
75ml (2½fl oz) olive oil
4 tomatoes, peeled, seeded and chopped
125ml (4fl oz) dry white wine
2kg (4lb) assorted fish and shellfish, including lobster, prawns, mussels and squid
salt
freshly ground black pepper
4 tblspn chopped fresh herbs
toasted Italian bread slices

1 Cook the onions, green pepper and garlic in the oil in a flameproof casserole until softened. Add the tomatoes and wine, bring to the boil, then simmer until the mixture thickens slightly.

2 Add the firmer seafood, with salt and pepper to taste. Cook for 5 minutes, stirring frequently.

3 Add tender seafood such as fish fillets, with shellfish. Cover with water and simmer until fish flakes easily when tested with the tip of a sharp knife. Discard any shellfish that have not opened. Stir in fresh herbs. Serve hot, straight from the casserole, ladling the stew over toasted bread in deep plates.
Serves 6

Kitchen Tip
This stew provides the perfect opportunity for visiting the fish market early in the morning to obtain the best of the catch of the day. Fresh fish will have clear, bright eyes, moist shiny skin, a fresh sea smell, and firm flesh. Buy shellfish from a reputable supplier and make sure that the shells are tightly closed.
  Don't ignore varieties of fish simply because they are unfamiliar; ask the fishmonger for advice on how to cook them.

EGGS AND CHEESE

Every nation has its own recipes for eggs and cheese, from simple omelettes to pies and bakes. This chapter explores some of the contributions made by Mediterranean countries, and includes gnocchi, a baked egg dish from Provence, and an Italian frittata.

Potato and Cheese Gnocchi

In Italy, where this dish originated, freshly grated Parmesan would be used instead of Emmental cheese.

1kg (2lb) potatoes, chopped
salt
125g (4oz) plain flour
375g (12oz) Emmental cheese, grated
30g (1oz) butter, melted

1 Bring a large saucepan of lightly salted water to the boil, add the potatoes and cook until very tender. Drain thoroughly, then mash with a fork or hand-held electric mixer, using a whipping action to create a fluffy texture. Beat in the flour, mixing well.

2 Rolls teaspoonfuls of the mixture into balls. Press each ball lightly with the prongs of a fork to flatten it slightly.

3 Preheat oven to 180°C (350°F/ Gas 4). Bring a saucepan of water to the boil, drop in a quarter of the gnocchi and cook until the gnocchi rise to the surface. As each gnocchi bobs up, remove it with a slotted spoon. Repeat with the remaining batches of gnocchi.

4 Place gnocchi and cheese in alternate layers in an ovenproof dish. Pour over the melted butter and bake for 15 minutes or until the topping is melted and bubbling. Serve at once.
Serves 6

Potato and Cheese Gnocchi

Spanish Omelette

2 tblspn olive oil
1 small potato, diced
¼ red pepper, chopped
¼ green pepper, chopped
½ onion, chopped
1 tomato, chopped
1 tblspn chopped fresh parsley
2 eggs, separated
1 tblspn water

1 Heat olive oil in a frying pan with a heatproof handle, add potato, pepper, onion, tomato and parsley and cook over moderate heat, turning frequently, until potatoes are tender and lightly browned.

2 Meanwhile, beat egg whites in a clean grease-free bowl until light and fluffy. Mix egg yolks with water, then fold in the egg whites.

3 Preheat grill. Pour egg mixture over vegetables in frying pan and cook over gentle heat until lightly set.

4 Place frying pan under grill and cook for 1 minute until firm and golden brown on top. Cut into wedges to serve.
Serves 2

Kitchen Tip
Instead of finishing the omelette off under the grill, it may be inverted onto a plate and returned to the frying pan. This is, however, quite a tricky operation and not to be recommended when you wish to impress.

Ricotta Balls

500g (1lb) ricotta cheese

3 rashers rindless streaky bacon, finely chopped

½ tspn grated nutmeg

4 tblspn chopped fresh parsley

2 tblspn mayonnaise

3 eggs, lightly beaten

125g (4oz) dried breadcrumbs

oil for deep frying

1 Combine ricotta, bacon, nutmeg, parsley, mayonnaise and eggs. Mix well.

2 Using about 1 tablespoon of mixture at a time, form balls. Roll in breadcrumbs to coat.

3 Heat the oil for deep frying in a medium saucepan over moderate heat. Fry ricotta balls in batches for about 2 minutes each. Drain and keep hot while frying the remainder. Serve.

Serves 4

Omelette Roll with Sautéed Vegetables

45g (1½ oz) butter

2 large eggs, lightly beaten

½ small potato, diced

1 small leek, white part only, finely sliced

¼ red pepper, finely chopped

1 Heat 15g/½oz of butter in an omelette pan over moderate heat until it sizzles. Add eggs, swirling pan so that they cover base. Cook until set, lifting edges of omelette to allow surplus mixture to flow underneath.

2 When cooked, ease omelette out of pan, using a spatula. Gently roll omelette up, cut it in half lengthwise, place halves on a warmed plate and keep hot.

3 Heat remaining butter in clean frying pan. Add potato and cook, stirring constantly, for 5 minutes. Add leek and pepper and cook for 2 minutes. Spoon vegetables over omelette.

Serves 1

Provençal Baked Eggs

1 large aubergine, cut into 1cm (½in) slices

125ml (4fl oz) vegetable oil

1 large onion, chopped

2 cloves garlic, crushed

4 large tomatoes, chopped

3 tblspn tomato purée

60ml (2fl oz) dry white wine

4 eggs

1 tblspn chopped fresh parsley

1 Preheat oven to 190°C (375°F/Gas 5). Rinse aubergine slices; pat dry then cut into small cubes.

2 Heat oil in a large frying pan, add onion and garlic and cook for 2 minutes. Add aubergine to frying pan and fry for 2 minutes, then stir in the tomatoes and tomato purée. Add wine and cook, stirring occasionally, for 10 minutes.

3 Spoon aubergine mixture into a shallow baking dish. Bake for 10 minutes. Remove from oven and make 4 depressions in vegetable mixture, using the back of a spoon.

4 Break an egg into each depression and sprinkle with parsley. Return baking dish to oven and cook until eggs are just set.

Serves 4

Ricotta Balls, Omelette Roll with Sautéed Vegetables

Parmesan Frittata

Spinach and Cheese Pie

125ml (4fl oz) olive oil

1 onion, finely chopped

250g (8oz) drained cooked spinach

200g (6½oz) feta cheese, crumbled

200g (6½oz) ricotta cheese

4 eggs, lightly beaten

2 tblspn grated Parmesan cheese

125ml (4fl oz) milk

grated nutmeg

freshly ground black pepper

10 sheets filo pastry

1 Preheat oven to 180°C (350°F/ Gas 4). Heat 2 tblspn of the oil in a medium frying pan, add the onion and cook until tender. Add the spinach and mix well.

2 Mash the feta cheese with the ricotta in a bowl. Add the eggs, Parmesan and milk, with the spinach mixture. Season to taste with nutmeg and pepper. Mix well.

3 Brush a 28 x 18cm (11 x 7in) baking dish with some of the remaining oil. Place 5 sheets of filo in the base, brushing each sheet in turn with oil, and letting the edges come up the sides of the dish.

4 Spread the filling evenly on top, fold over the edges of the filo sheets and cover with the remaining sheets of filo, brushing each with oil as before. Tuck the edges of the filo down the sides of the dish. Brush the top of the pie with oil.

5 Bake for about 40 minutes or until the pie is crisp and golden. Allow to cool slightly, then cut into squares and serve.
Serves 8

Kitchen Tip
Always cover any sheets of filo not being used with a damp tea towel to prevent them from drying out.

Parmesan Frittata

2 onions, chopped

60ml (2fl oz) olive oil

250g (8oz) boiled potato, cubed

100g (3½oz) sliced salami, chopped

1 red pepper, chopped

6 eggs, lightly beaten

125ml (4fl oz) milk

freshly ground black pepper

4 tblspn grated Parmesan cheese

1 Preheat oven to 180°C (350°F/ Gas 4). Sauté the onions in the olive oil in a large frying pan until tender. Add the potato, salami and red pepper; cook for 3 minutes, stirring constantly. Cool slightly, then stir in the eggs, milk, pepper and Parmesan.

2 Pour the mixture into a greased ovenproof dish and bake for 25 minutes or until set. Serve at once.
Serves 4

Pasta, Rice and Polenta

Pasta and rice are the basis of some of the most delicious dishes to emerge from the Mediterranean region. Together with polenta, that flat cake made from cooked cornmeal, they provide the perfect vehicle for a range of superb sauces.

Fettucine with Broad Beans, Red Peppers and Grainy Mustard

500g (1lb) red peppers
350ml (12fl oz) chicken stock
315g (10oz) shelled broad beans
salt
1 onion, chopped
3 tblspn grainy mustard
30g (1oz) butter
500g (1lb) thin fettucine
freshly ground black pepper

1 Char the red peppers over a gas flame or under a hot grill until blackened on all sides. Place them in a paper bag and allow to steam for 10-15 minutes, then remove peel and seeds and cut pepper flesh into 5mm (1/4in) wide strips. Set aside.

2 Heat the stock in a heavy-based saucepan until simmering. Add the broad beans with salt to taste and cook for about 6 minutes until tender. Add onion and mustard and simmer for 1 minute more, then add butter and pepper strips. Simmer, stirring gently, for 2 minutes.

3 Meanwhile cook the fettucine in boiling salted water until tender or *al dente*. Drain. Transfer to pan with broad bean mixture. Toss well, season with black pepper and serve at once.
Serves 6-8

Spirelli with Tomato and Artichoke Sauce

1 tblspn olive oil
1 onion, chopped
2 cloves garlic, crushed
4 large ripe tomatoes, peeled and chopped
2 tblspn chopped fresh basil
2 tblspn chopped fresh parsley
1 x 425g (13 1/2oz) can artichoke hearts, drained and halved
375g (12oz) spirelli (pasta spirals)
basil sprig and grated Parmesan cheese to serve

1 Heat the oil in a saucepan, add the onion and garlic and fry gently until tender. Stir in the tomatoes, basil and parsley. Bring to the boil, lower the heat and simmer for about 30 minutes until the sauce has reduced and thickened. Stir in the artichoke halves.

2 Cook the spirelli in boiling salted water until tender or *al dente*. Drain well. Top with the sauce. Garnish with basil and serve with grated Parmesan.
Serves 4

Spirelli with Tomato and Artichoke Sauce

Spaghetti with Raw Tomatoes and Herbs

750g (1½lb) ripe tomatoes, seeded and cubed

30g (1oz) mixed fresh herbs, including basil, chopped

500g (1lb) spaghetti

salt

125ml (4fl oz) olive oil

freshly ground black pepper

1 Combine tomatoes and herbs in a heatproof serving bowl.

2 Cook spaghetti in boiling salted water until *al dente*. Drain.

3 Heat olive oil in a small frying pan until it is very hot. Immediately pour oil over the tomatoes and herbs. Season and mix well.

4 Add hot pasta to bowl, toss and serve at once.
Serves 4

Tagliatelle and Potatoes with Garlic and Oil

2 large baking potatoes

375g (12oz) tagliatelle

salt

250ml (8fl oz) olive oil

10 garlic cloves, crushed

1 red chilli, seeded and chopped

freshly ground black pepper

4 tblspn chopped fresh parsley

1 Preheat oven to 200°C (400°F/ Gas 6). Bake potatoes for 40-50 minutes or until tender. When cool, cut into 5mm (¼in) slices

2 Cook tagliatelle in boiling salted water until *al dente;* drain.

3 Heat oil in a large saucepan. Add garlic, chilli and potatoes and cook over moderate heat for 5 minutes until golden.

4 Add tagliatelle to pan and mix. Season. Serve hot, sprinkled with chopped parsley.
Serves 6

Sausage and Pancetta Risotto

Sausage and Pancetta Risotto

2 tblspn olive oil

90g (3oz) pancetta or rindless back bacon, chopped

1 small carrot, sliced

1 onion, thinly sliced

2 x 410g (13oz) cans chopped tomatoes

600ml (1pt) chicken stock

185g (6oz) drained canned kidney beans

30g (1oz) butter

4 Italian sausages, casings removed

½ tspn dried sage

½ tspn dried rosemary

2 cloves garlic, crushed

185g (6oz) Arborio rice

125ml (4fl oz) red wine

½ red or yellow pepper, roughly chopped

90g (3oz) grated Parmesan cheese

1 Heat oil in a large frying pan, add pancetta or bacon, carrot and onion and fry for 10 minutes, stirring occasionally. Stir in tomatoes, lower heat and simmer for 15 minutes. Stir in stock and beans, remove pan from heat and set aside.

2 In a saucepan, melt butter and fry sausages with sage, rosemary and garlic for 7 minutes, stirring frequently until sausage is crumbly.

3 Add rice and wine. Stir mixture until liquid has evaporated, then add 250ml (8fl oz) of bean/stock mixture. Cook until liquid has evaporated.

4 Continue adding bean/stock mixture in this fashion until all liquid has been absorbed and rice is tender, about 20 minutes. Stir in chopped pepper and Parmesan.
Serves 4

Wild Rice and Mushrooms

30g (1oz) butter

4 spring onions, chopped

1 leek, white part only, finely sliced

125g (4oz) button mushrooms, sliced

250g (8oz) wild rice, washed and drained

600ml (1pt) chicken stock

1 Melt butter in a large frying pan. Add spring onions, leek and mushrooms. Cook over moderate heat for 3 minutes, stirring frequently. Remove with a slotted spoon and set aside.

2 Add wild rice to butter remaining in pan and stir until well coated. Add stock, bring to the boil, then simmer for 30-40 minutes until rice is cooked and the liquid has been absorbed.

3 Stir in spring onions, leek slices and mushrooms. Heat and serve.
Serves 4

Polenta with Mushroom Sauce

300ml (10fl oz) milk
300ml (10fl oz) water
1 tspn crushed black peppercorns
2 cloves garlic, crushed
125g (4oz) polenta
30g (1oz) grated Parmesan cheese
2 tspn oil
1 onion, chopped
125g (4oz) mushrooms, sliced
1/4 tspn ground chilli powder
250g (8oz) canned chopped tomatoes
thyme sprig for garnish

1 Combine the milk, water, pepper and half the garlic in a small saucepan. Bring to the boil, remove from the heat, cover and set aside for 20 minutes. Strain the milk into a medium saucepan.

2 Add the polenta and stir over moderate heat until boiling, then simmer, still stirring, for 10-15 minutes, until mixture starts to come away from the sides of pan.

3 Spoon the polenta into a greased and lined 20cm (8in) round baking dish or tray, spread it evenly and set aside to cool.

4 Preheat oven to 180°C (350°F/Gas 4). Sprinkle the polenta with the cheese. Bake for 15 minutes, cut into serving wedges and place on a serving plate. Keep hot.

5 Make the sauce. Heat the oil in a medium frying pan, add the onion, remaining garlic, mushrooms and chilli powder and cook for 3 minutes. Stir in the tomatoes and cook for 3 minutes more. Pour the sauce into a serving bowl and serve with the polenta, garnished with the thyme sprig.
Serves 4

Variation
Fry 2 chopped rindless streaky bacon rashers with onion and garlic mixture. Omit chilli powder.

Risotto with Ham and Lemon

1 lemon, rind only, cut in fine strips
900ml (1 1/2pt) chicken stock
30g (1oz) butter
1 Spanish onion, finely chopped
1 clove garlic, bruised
60g (2oz) cooked ham, chopped
1 sprig fresh thyme
250g (8oz) Arborio rice
125ml (4fl oz) dry white wine
60g (2oz) grated Parmesan cheese

1 Blanch the lemon rind in boiling water for a few seconds. Drain and set aside. Heat the stock to simmering point in a large saucepan; have a large ladle handy.

2 Melt half the butter in a large heavy-based saucepan. Add onion and saute until transparent. Stir in garlic and ham and cook for 2 minutes more, then remove garlic and add thyme and rice. Stir constantly until grains of rice are transparent, then add wine and cook, stirring constantly, until liquid is absorbed.

3 Add a ladleful of hot stock to pan. Cook, stirring constantly, until absorbed. Keep adding stock in this manner until all stock has been absorbed and rice is tender but still firm to the bite. The entire process should take about 20 minutes.

4 Stir in Parmesan, strips of lemon rind and remaining butter. Cook for 5 minutes more.
Serves 4

Polenta with Mushroom Sauce, Wild Rice and Mushrooms

Meat and Poultry

In many Mediterranean countries, meat is regarded as a luxury item, to be treated with respect. In Italy, tender cuts such as veal escalopes are sealed quickly in hot oil, then cooked until perfectly tender before being served with a sauce made from the pan juices. The French excel at slow cooked dishes like the Provençal Daube de Boeuf, while in Greece it is lamb that is the favoured meat.

Beef with Sun-dried Tomatoes

1/2 x 170g (5 1/2oz) jar sun-dried tomatoes in oil, drained, 4 tblspn oil reserved

500g (1lb) thinly sliced rump steak, cut into thin strips

2 tblspn olive oil

1 red onion, chopped

2 cloves garlic, crushed

1 tomato, finely chopped

220g (7oz) pattypan squash, quartered, or courgettes, sliced

2 tspn finely chopped fresh rosemary

2 tblspn tomato purée

350ml (12fl oz) chicken stock

60ml (2fl oz) white wine

1 tspn cornflour

1 tblspn finely chopped fresh parsley

1 Heat the oil from the sun-dried tomatoes in a medium frying pan. Add the beef. Cook over high heat for 2-3 minutes, then remove with a slotted spoon and set aside.

2 Add the olive oil to the frying pan. When hot, add the onion, garlic, tomato, squash or courgettes, rosemary and tomato purée. Cook for 2 minutes.

3 Combine the stock, wine and cornflour in a jug. Add to the frying pan and cook, stirring, for about 10 minutes, until reduced by half.

4 Stir in the beef strips, sun-dried tomatoes and parsley. Heat through for 1-2 minutes. Serve.
Serves 4

Veal with Mushroom and Parmesan Cream Sauce

If preferred, substitute chicken breasts for the veal escalopes.

60g (2oz) dried porcini mushrooms

6 veal escalopes, about 500g (1lb)

300ml (10fl oz) single cream

155g (5oz) grated Parmesan cheese

salt

freshly ground black pepper

2 eggs, beaten

60g (2oz) butter

1 Soak the mushrooms in warm water to cover for 30 minutes. Drain and chop. Beat the veal escalopes with a mallet to flatten.

2 Combine the mushrooms, cream and 90g (3oz) of the Parmesan in a saucepan. Cook over moderate heat for 15 minutes. Add salt and freshly ground black pepper to taste. Cover and keep warm.

3 In a deep plate combine the beaten eggs with the remaining Parmesan and a little salt to taste. Dip the escalopes in this mixture, turning to coat them well.

4 Heat the butter in a large frying pan. When foamy, add the escalopes and cook until golden brown on both sides.

5 Transfer the escalopes to a heated platter, pour the mushroom cream sauce over the top and serve at once.
Serves 6

Veal Piccata

30g (1oz) flour

8 medium veal escalopes, tenderized

60g (2oz) butter

125ml (4fl oz) lemon juice

125ml (4fl oz) dry white wine

1 lemon, thinly sliced, for garnish

1 Lightly flour the veal escalopes on both sides. Shake off excess.

2 Melt the butter in a medium frying pan over moderate heat. When the butter bubbles, add the veal escalopes and saute for about 2 minutes on each side. When the veal is almost cooked, sprinkle on the lemon juice. Using tongs or a fish slice, transfer the escalopes to a serving dish; keep hot.

3 Add the wine to the frying pan and boil over high heat, stirring constantly until the liquid is reduced to about 125ml (4fl oz). Pour the sauce over the veal.

4 Cut the lemon into paper thin slices and place 3 slices on each escalope. Serve immediately.
Serves 4

Beef with Sun-dried Tomatoes, Veal Piccata

Lamb and Lemon Kebabs with Yogurt

Lamb and Lemon Kebabs with Yogurt

60ml (2fl oz) olive oil

2 cloves garlic, crushed

2 tspn ground cumin

1 tspn paprika

75ml (2½fl oz) lemon juice

1 tspn finely grated lemon rind

60ml (2fl oz) coconut cream

750g (1½lb) lean lamb, cut into 2cm (¾in) cubes

1 tblspn chopped fresh parsley

250ml (8fl oz) natural low fat yogurt

1 tblspn chopped fresh mint

1 Combine oil, garlic, cumin, paprika, lemon juice, lemon rind and coconut cream in a large non-metallic bowl. Add lamb. Mix well, cover, chill and marinate for at least 6 hours and up to 24 hours.

2 Preheat grill. Thread lamb onto skewers; grill under moderate heat for 3 minutes each side or until cooked. Sprinkle with parsley. Combine yogurt and mint. Serve with kebabs.

Serves 6

Moussaka

1kg (2lb) aubergine

salt

125-150ml (4-5fl oz) olive oil

1 onion, thinly sliced

750g (1½lb) lean minced lamb

1 x 410g (13oz) can chopped tomatoes, drained

2 small cloves garlic, crushed

4 tblspn chopped fresh parsley

freshly ground black pepper

90g (3oz) grated Kefalotyri or Parmesan cheese

Sauce

30g (1oz) butter

30g (1oz) flour

600ml (1pt) hot milk

grated nutmeg

2 eggs

1 Cut the aubergine into 1cm (½in) slices. Place in a colander and sprinkle liberally with salt. Leave to drain for 30 minutes to draw out the bitter juices. Rinse under cold running water; drain on paper towels.

2 Heat 30ml (1fl oz) of the oil in a flameproof casserole, add the onion and sauté for about 5 minutes until golden. Add the minced lamb and cook, stirring frequently, until browned. Stir in the tomatoes, garlic and parsley, with salt and pepper to taste. Lower the heat and simmer the mixture for 15-20 minutes, until slightly thickened.

3 Preheat oven to 180°C (350°F/Gas 4). Heat 90ml (3fl oz) of the remaining oil in a large frying pan, add the aubergine slices in batches and fry until golden brown on both sides. Remove with a slotted spoon and drain on paper towels. Add more oil to the frying pan if necessary.

4 Set aside 30g (1oz) of the cheese for the topping. Arrange a layer of aubergine slices in the base of a baking dish. Add a layer of meat, then a sprinkling of grated cheese. Repeat the layers until all the ingredients except the reserved cheese have been used, ending with a layer of aubergine.

5 Make the sauce. Melt the butter in a saucepan. Add the flour and cook for 2 minutes, stirring constantly. Gradually add the milk, stirring all the time until the sauce boils and thickens. Season to taste with salt, pepper and nutmeg. Lower the heat and simmer the sauce for 5 minutes, then remove from the heat.

6 Beat the eggs in a bowl. Whisk in about 60ml (2fl oz) of the sauce, then tip the contents of the bowl into the pan, whisking until well mixed.

7 Spoon the sauce over the top layer of aubergine slices. Sprinkle with the reserved cheese and bake for about 45 minutes, until bubbly and golden brown. Allow to stand for 10 minutes at room temperature before serving.

Serves 6

Kitchen Tip

Leaving the moussaka to stand at room temperature immediately after cooking allows the mixture to firm up and makes it easier to cut and serve.

Veal with Mozzarella

60g (2oz) butter

4 veal escalopes, tenderized

60ml (2fl oz) dry white wine

1 x 410g (13oz) can chopped tomatoes

1 tspn finely chopped fresh basil

375g (12oz) mozzarella cheese, thinly sliced

1 Preheat oven to 190°C (375°F/Gas 5). Heat the butter in a large frying pan, add the veal escalopes and cook over moderate heat for 1 minute on each side. Using a fish slice, transfer the veal to a baking dish and keep hot.

2 Add the wine to the butter remaining in the frying pan and cook until reduced by half. Add the tomatoes and basil and cook over moderate heat for 5 minutes.

3 Pour the tomato sauce over the veal in the baking dish. Cover with the sliced mozzarella and bake for 10 minutes or until the cheese melts. Serve.
Serves 4

Veal and Cheese Bundles

75g (2½oz) mozzarella cheese

75g (2½oz) rindless streaky bacon

2 tblspn chopped fresh parsley

2 tblspn grated Parmesan cheese

4 veal escalopes, tenderized

60g (2oz) flour

60ml (2fl oz) oil

185ml (6fl oz) dry white wine

1 Finely chop mozzarella, bacon and parsley in a blender or food processor. Transfer mixture to a bowl and stir in Parmesan.

2 Spoon one quarter of mixture onto each veal escalope. Roll up to make a neat bundle enclosing the filling; tie with string. Roll bundles in flour.

3 Heat oil in a large frying pan, add veal bundles and fry until lightly browned. Add wine and cook over moderate heat for 5 minutes.

Remove string from bundles and place on a serving dish. Strain pan juices over and serve.
Serves 4

Pork and Herb Patties with Aubergine Sauce

500g (1lb) lean minced pork

2 spring onions, finely chopped

2 cloves garlic, crushed

2 tblspn chopped fresh coriander

30g (1oz) fresh breadcrumbs

1 egg, beaten

2 tblspn oil

250g (8oz) aubergine, peeled and diced, steamed until tender

2 tspn ground cumin

¼ tspn salt

¼ tspn freshly ground black pepper

60ml (2fl oz) soured cream

1 Combine the minced pork, spring onions, garlic, coriander, breadcrumbs and egg in a medium bowl. Mix well. Form into 8 patties, about 2cm (¾in) thick.

2 Heat the oil in a medium nonstick frying pan over moderate heat. Add the patties in batches, frying them for 3-4 minutes on each side or until cooked through. Drain on paper towels and transfer to a serving plate. Keep hot.

3 Purée the steamed aubergine with the cumin, salt and pepper in a blender or food processor. Transfer the puree to a small saucepan, stir in the soured cream and heat gently until just warmed through. Do not allow the mixture to boil. Serve the sauce over the patties and garnish with thin strips of red pepper, if liked.
Serves 4

Pork and Herb Patties with Aubergine Sauce

Lamb Stew with Lemon Sauce

1 shoulder of lamb, boned
2 onions, chopped
1 red pepper, chopped
2 sticks celery, sliced
600ml (1pt) chicken stock
45g (1½ oz) butter
2 tblspn flour
2 egg yolks
60ml (2fl oz) lemon juice
dill sprig for garnish

1 Slice the lamb into 2cm (¾in) cubes, discarding any fat. Place the cubes in a large saucepan with the onions, pepper and celery. Add the stock. Bring to the boil; skim until the surface is clear. Cover and simmer for 1-1½ hours until tender.

2 Using a slotted spoon, transfer the meat and vegetables to a deep serving dish; keep hot. Strain the stock into a measuring jug, reserving 350ml (12fl oz).

3 Melt the butter in a medium saucepan. Add the flour and stir over moderate heat for 2 minutes. Gradually add the measured stock, stirring until the mixture boils and thickens slightly. Lower the heat to a simmer.

4 In a bowl, whisk the egg yolks with the lemon juice. Pour in about 60ml (2fl oz) of the hot stock mixture and whisk until smooth. Tip the contents of the bowl into the pan containing the stock mixture and stir constantly over a low heat until the mixture thickens further; do not allow it to approach boiling point. Pour the sauce over the meat. Garnish with dill and serve.

Serves 6

Lamb Stew with Lemon Sauce, Veal Rolls in Tomato Sauce

Daube de Boeuf

This is a traditional beef stew from Provence in the South of France.

2kg (4lb) lean stewing beef, cut into 5cm (2in) cubes
2 large onions, sliced
4 carrots, thickly sliced
1 stalk celery, thickly sliced
2 cloves garlic, crushed
4 parsley sprigs
2 bay leaves
1 tblspn crumbled fresh thyme or 1 tspn dried thyme
60ml (2fl oz) brandy
1 bottle full-bodied red wine
3 tblspn olive oil
4 cloves
1 tspn black peppercorns
60g (2oz) butter
500g (1lb) button mushrooms, sliced
1 tblspn tomato purée
grated rind and juice of 1 orange
salt
freshly ground black pepper

1 Combine beef, onions, carrots, celery, garlic, parsley, bay leaves, thyme, brandy, wine and 2 tlbspn oil in a large non-metallic bowl. Tie cloves and peppercorns in a piece of muslin and add to bowl. Cover; refrigerate for 24 hours, stirring occasionally.

2 Remove bowl from refrigerator and allow contents to come to room temperature. Remove beef with a slotted spoon, dry thoroughly on paper towels and set aside. Remove vegetables from marinade in the same way; reserve.

3 Pour marinade (with muslin spice bag) into a flameproof casserole. Boil until reduced by one quarter; remove from the heat.

4 Melt butter with remaining olive oil in a large frying pan over high heat. When foam subsides add beef in batches, frying until brown on all sides. Using a slotted spoon, transfer beef to casserole with marinade.

5 Add reserved vegetables to frying pan and sauté for 6 minutes until golden. Using a slotted spoon, transfer to casserole. Add mushrooms to pan; fry for 4 minutes. Set aside.

6 Stir tomato purée into casserole. Simmer, covered, for 3-4 hours until meat is very tender. Stir in reserved mushrooms, orange rind and juice. Season. Remove spice bag and bay leaves.

Serves 8

Veal Rolls in Tomato Sauce

4 thin slices prosciutto
4 veal escalopes, tenderized
60g (2oz) grated Parmesan cheese
60g (2oz) butter
2 tblspn oil
250ml (8fl oz) dry Marsala
250g (8oz) canned tomatoes, puréed
1 tblspn chopped fresh parsley
1 clove garlic, crushed
parsley or coriander sprig for garnish

1 Lay a slice of prosciutto on each veal escalope, sprinkle with 1 tspn of Parmesan and roll up. Secure rolls with cocktail sticks.

2 Heat butter with oil in a large frying pan. Add veal rolls and cook until golden on all sides.

3 Stir in Marsala and cook, uncovered, until wine is reduced by half. Transfer veal rolls to a serving dish and keep hot.

4 Add puréed tomatoes, parsley and garlic to wine remaining in frying pan. Cook over moderate heat for 5 minutes until sauce has thickened slightly.

5 Pour sauce onto serving plate. Slice veal rolls and arrange on sauce. Garnish and serve.

Serves 4

Chicken, Tomato and Pimiento Casserole

60ml (2fl oz) oil

4 chicken breast fillets, cut into thin strips

1 turnip, cut into thin strips

2 onions, chopped

1 x 470g (15oz) can pimientos, drained, cut into strips

250ml (8fl oz) dry white wine

1 x 410g (13oz) can chopped tomatoes

3 tblspn chopped fresh basil

basil leaves for garnish

1 Heat the oil in a large frying pan, add the chicken strips and cook over moderate heat for 2 minutes, stirring constantly. Using a slotted spoon, transfer the chicken to a bowl and set aside.

2 Add the turnips, onion and pimientos to the oil remaining in the pan. Cook for 2-3 minutes.

3 Stir the wine and tomatoes into the pan, bring to the boil, then lower the heat and simmer for 10 minutes. Do not cover the pan.

4 Stir in the chicken and basil, heat through for 1 minute, then serve. Garnish with basil leaves, if liked.
Serves 4

Chicken Marsala

75g (2½oz) butter

4 chicken breast fillets, sliced in half horizontally

60g (2oz) flour

salt

freshly ground black pepper

75ml (2½fl oz) Marsala

3 tblspn snipped chives

1 Heat 45g (1½oz) of the butter in a heavy-based frying pan until foaming. Dredge the chicken in flour, shaking off excess, add to the pan and cook for 1 minute on each side until golden brown.

Chicken, Tomato and Pimiento Casserole

Using tongs, transfer to a bowl, season with salt and pepper and keep hot.

2 Pour off all but 1 tablespoon of the butter from the pan. Add the Marsala and boil for 1 minute, scraping up any sediment on the base of the pan. Add the remaining butter, with any juices from the reserved chicken.

3 Stir the sauce over moderate heat until it thickens. Return the chicken to the pan and simmer until cooked through, basting frequently with the sauce. Serve.
Serves 4

Grilled Mustard Poussins

4 poussins, about 750g (1½lb) each

125ml (4fl oz) white wine

125ml (4fl oz) olive oil

2 tblspn chopped fresh parsley

few sprigs of lemon thyme

1 onion, sliced

freshly ground black pepper

salt

4 tblspn Dijon mustard

60g (2oz) butter, melted

1 Split the birds by cutting along the backbone on either side. Discard the backbone or save for stock. Open birds out flat and place in a large roasting tin.

2 Combine the wine, oil, parsley, thyme and onion. Pour over the poussins, turning to coat them in the mixture. Sprinkle with plenty of black pepper. Cover and refrigerate overnight, turning poussins from time to time.

3 Preheat grill to high. Remove birds from marinade and season with salt. Coat each bird with mustard and brush with melted butter. Grill breast down for 5 minutes, turn and grill for 10-15 minutes more or until cooked through. Baste frequently with remaining butter and mustard. Serve hot.
Serves 4

Vegetables and Salads

Visit any Mediterranean market and marvel at the colourful array of vegetables. Deep purple aubergines, red, green and yellow peppers, beefsteak tomatoes, bunches of glossy green spinach - the selection may lack the cool crispness of some northern varieties, but it is an open invitation to create a meal that looks as good as it tastes.

Buttered Beans and Pinenuts

750g (1½lb) green beans

60g (2oz) butter

60g (2oz) pinenuts

1 tblspn lemon juice

1 Top and tail the beans; cut them into 4cm (1½in) lengths. Boil or steam until tender. Drain thoroughly.

2 Melt the butter in a frying pan, add the pinenuts and stir fry until pale golden brown. Add the beans and lemon juice and stir until heated through. Serve.
Serves 4

Glazed Honey Onions

20 pearl onions or shallots

60g (2oz) butter

2 tblspn clear honey

1 Peel the onions; cut them in half if large.

2 Bring a saucepan of water to the boil, add the onions and cook for 5 minutes. Remove with a slotted spoon and set aside.

3 Heat the butter with the honey in a large frying pan over gentle heat. When the mixture bubbles, add the onions and cook for 5-10 minutes until golden brown and tender. Serve.
Serves 4-6

Fennel with Parmesan

3 small fennel bulbs, quartered

250ml (8fl oz) water

60g (2oz) butter

salt

freshly ground black pepper

60g (2oz) grated Parmesan cheese

1 Place fennel in a saucepan with measured water. Add butter and bring to boil. Lower heat and simmer, covered, until fennel is tender when pierced.

2 Transfer contents of the pan to a heated serving dish. Season with salt and pepper and stir in Parmesan. Serve hot.
Serves 4

Pommes Patricia

60ml (2fl oz) olive oil

2 cloves garlic, crushed

3 tspn ground cumin

½ tspn freshly ground black pepper

6 medium potatoes, cut into 2cm (¾in) cubes

2 red onions, cut into 2cm (¾in) squares

2 tspn chopped fresh parsley

Preheat oven to 190°C (375°F/Gas 5). Mix oil, garlic, cumin and pepper in a large bowl. Add potatoes and onions and stir to coat. Tip mixture into a roasting tin and roast for 30 minutes or until the potatoes are crisp and golden. Stir in parsley.
Serves 4

Pommes Patricia

Ratatouille

- 75ml (2½fl oz) olive oil
- 2 large onions, cut into eighths
- 1 large aubergine, sliced
- 4 firm tomatoes, peeled, seeded and roughly chopped
- 4 large courgettes, cut into 2cm (¾in) slices
- 2 peppers, red and green, cut into strips
- 3 cloves garlic, crushed
- salt
- freshly ground black pepper

1 Heat in a flameproof casserole, add onions and cook for 10 minutes over gentle heat until golden.

2 Cut aubergine slices into quarters and add to casserole with tomatoes, courgettes, peppers and garlic. Season.

3 Cover and simmer for 30 minutes or until all vegetables are tender and oil absorbed. Serve hot or cold.
Serves 4

Ricotta and Hazelnut Stuffed Potatoes

- 4 large baking potatoes, scrubbed
- 2 tspn oil
- 125g (4oz) ricotta cheese
- 2 tblspn grated Parmesan cheese
- 4 canned asparagus spears, chopped
- 1 tblspn snipped chives
- 2 tblspn chopped hazelnuts

1 Preheat oven to 200°C (400°F/Gas 6). Prick potatoes all over. Place in oven and bake for 1-1¼ hours until tender.

2 Cut potatoes in half. Scoop flesh into a bowl, leaving a 1cm (½in) thick potato shell. Using oil, brush potato shells inside and out. Arrange on a baking sheet; return to oven for 10 minutes.

3 Mash potato flesh with ricotta and Parmesan. Stir in asparagus and chives.

Potato and Courgette Bake

4 Spoon filling into potato shells. Top with hazelnuts. Return to oven for 15-20 minutes to heat.
Serves 4

Potato and Courgette Bake

- 500g (1lb) potatoes, cut into large chunks
- 2 tblspn oil
- 4 courgettes, sliced
- 1 onion, chopped
- 2 cloves garlic, crushed
- 4 tomatoes, chopped
- 1 tblspn chopped fresh basil
- 2 tspn chopped fresh oregano
- 60g (2oz) fresh wholemeal breadcrumbs
- 60g (2oz) grated Parmesan or mature Cheddar cheese

1 Preheat oven to 180°C (350°F/Gas 4). Cook potatoes in boiling salted water until tender. Drain; spoon into 4 serving dishes.

2 Heat half the oil in a frying pan, add courgettes and stir fry until tender. Add to the potatoes.

3 Heat remaining oil in frying pan, add onion and garlic and sauté until tender. Add tomatoes, basil and oregano and cook until pulpy. Pour over potato and courgette mixture.

4 Combine breadcrumbs and cheese and sprinkle over bakes. Cook for 30 minutes until the topping is golden.
Serves 4

Provençal Aubergines

2 large aubergines, halved lengthwise

salt

2 tblspn olive oil

1 onion, chopped

2 garlic cloves, crushed

2 rashers rindless streaky bacon, chopped, optional

90g (3oz) canned chopped tomatoes

1 tspn chopped fresh thyme

1 egg

60g (2oz) dried breadcrumbs

125g (4oz) cooked rice

60g (2oz) grated Parmesan cheese

1 Scoop flesh from aubergines, leaving a 2cm (³/₄in) thick shell. Sprinkle with salt and invert on paper towels. Set aside for 15 minutes. Combine remaining ingredients.

2 Preheat oven to 180°C (350°F/ Gas 4). Rinse aubergine shells and pat dry. Spoon filling into aubergine shells, arrange on a baking sheet and bake for 30 minutes. Serve hot.
Serves 4

Greek Haricot Beans with Vegetables

250g (8oz) haricot beans, soaked overnight in water to cover

1 onion, chopped

2 carrots, thinly sliced

2 sticks celery, thinly sliced

salt

1 tblspn tomato purée

125ml (4fl oz) olive oil

1 tspn chopped fresh sage

1 tspn chopped fresh rosemary

freshly ground black pepper

4 tblspn chopped fresh parsley

1 lemon, quartered

1 Drain beans and place in a large saucepan with fresh water to cover. Bring to boil and boil vigorously for 10 minutes, then lower heat and simmer for 40 minutes until tender. Drain.

2 Combine onion, carrots and celery in a saucepan. Add lightly salted water to cover. Bring to the boil, lower heat and simmer for 20 minutes or until vegetables are tender. Drain.

3 Combine beans and vegetables in a clean pan. Add tomato purée, oil, sage and rosemary. Season. Heat gently, turning mixture to coat. Place in serving dish, garnish with parsley and lemon.
Serves 4

Turkish Artichoke and Potato Casserole

4 fresh globe artichokes, trimmed, halved, chokes removed

juice of 1 lemon

125ml (4fl oz) olive oil

400ml (14fl oz) water

4 potatoes, halved

8 pearl onions or shallots, peeled but left whole

1 stick celery, cut into 2.5cm (1in) lengths

salt

1 tblspn cornflour

4 tblspn chopped fresh dill

1 Drop artichokes into a bowl of water mixed with half lemon juice. Set aside for 10 minutes.

2 Combine oil and water in a saucepan large enough to hold vegetables in a single layer. Bring to the boil. Add drained artichokes, potatoes, onions or shallots, celery and remaining lemon juice. Season.

3 Simmer vegetables for 45 minutes or until tender, shaking pan from time to time. Add a little more water if necessary.

4 Mix cornflour with water. Stir into vegetable mixture over moderate heat until sauce thickens. Add dill. Transfer artichoke and potato casserole to a serving dish.
Serves 4

Provençal Aubergines

35

Salad Niçoise

250g (8oz) green beans, trimmed

1 x 200g (6½oz) can tuna in oil, drained

125g (4oz) cherry tomatoes, quartered

4 hard-boiled eggs, sliced

12 pitted black olives

8 canned anchovy fillets, drained

1 tblspn snipped chives

1 tblspn drained capers

2 tblspn olive oil

2 tblspn French dressing

1 clove garlic, crushed

1 Bring a medium saucepan of water to the boil over moderate heat. Add the beans and cook for 1 minute; drain. Refresh under cold water, drain again and set aside.

2 Break up the tuna into bite-sized chunks. Arrange the beans, tuna, tomatoes, egg slices, olives and anchovy fillets on a serving platter.

3 Sprinkle with chives and capers and dress with a mixture of the olive oil, French dressing and crushed garlic.
Serves 4

Broad Bean Salad

salt

500g (1lb) shelled broad beans, thawed if frozen

150ml (5fl oz) natural low fat yogurt

3 tblspn mayonnaise

1 tblspn snipped chives

1 Bring a large saucepan of lightly salted water to the boil, add the broad beans and cook for about 7 minutes or until tender.

2 Drain the beans and mix while still warm with the yogurt, mayonnaise and chives. Cool before serving.
Serves 4

Endive and Mangetout Salad

200g (6½oz) mangetout, topped and tailed

1 curly endive, leaves torn into bite-sized pieces

1 orange, sliced and cut into small wedges

3 tblspn freshly squeezed orange juice

2 tspn finely grated orange rind

1 tblspn freshly squeezed lime juice

1 tblspn olive oil

2 tspn finely chopped fresh parsley

¼ tspn crushed black peppercorns

1 Bring a medium saucepan of water to the boil, add the mangetout and blanch for 30 seconds. Remove with a slotted spoon and refresh under cold water. Drain thoroughly.

2 Arrange the endive leaves, mangetout and orange wedges in a salad bowl. Whisk the remaining ingredients together in a small bowl or jug, pour over the salad, toss lightly and serve.
Serves 4

Fennel Salad

2 fennel bulbs

Dressing

2 tblspn olive oil

1 tblspn lemon juice

2 tblspn chopped fresh parsley

1 tblspn snipped chives

salt

freshly ground black pepper

1 Cut the fennel bulbs crosswise into 5mm (¼in) slices. Separate the rings and place them in a salad bowl.

2 Make the dressing by mixing the oil, lemon juice, parsley and chives, with salt and pepper to taste, in a screwtop jar. Close tightly; shake until well combined.

3 Pour the dressing over the fennel, toss lightly and serve.
Serves 4

Sweet Pimiento Salad

Illustrated on page 46

1 x 470g (15oz) can pimientos, drained

60ml (2fl oz) olive oil

1 tblspn red wine vinegar

1 tblspn lemon juice

1 tblspn clear honey

1 tblspn yellow mustard seeds

1 Slice pimientos into thin strips and arrange in a shallow dish.

2 Whisk olive oil, vinegar, lemon juice and honey together in a bowl or jug, stir in mustard seeds and pour over pimientos.

3 Cover dish. Chill the salad for at least 3 hours before serving to allow flavours to blend.
Serves 3-4

Radicchio and Pinenut Salad

1 red pepper

250g (8oz) broccoli florets

1 radicchio lettuce, shredded

4 tblspn pinenuts, toasted

4 tblspn olive oil

2 tblspn red wine vinegar

1 tblspn lemon juice

¼ tspn crushed black peppercorns

1 Cut the red pepper into very fine strips. Place them in a bowl of iced water and refrigerate for 15 minutes until they curl.

2 Meanwhile, bring a large saucepan of water to boil, add broccoli and blanch for 1 minute. Drain, refresh under cold water and drain again. Arrange lettuce on a serving platter, top with broccoli and add pinenuts.

3 Whisk olive oil, vinegar, lemon juice and crushed peppercorns in a bowl. Pour dressing over broccoli mixture and toss lightly. Drain red pepper curls and garnish the salad.
Serves 4

Salad Niçoise

DESSERTS

Desserts are not a universal feature of Mediterranean meals; in Greece, for instance it is customary to enjoy sweet treats like baklava with coffee in the late afternoon; if a sweet is served at all after lunch or dinner it is likely to be fresh fruit. However, the leisurely approach to the Mediterranean meal means that there is plenty of time for sweet endings.

Peaches in Wine

250ml (8fl oz) red wine

2 tblspn caster sugar

2.5cm (1in) stick cinnamon

2 cloves

grated rind of 1 lemon

6 peaches

1 Combine the wine, sugar, cinnamon, cloves and lemon rind in a large serving bowl. Stir until the sugar has dissolved.

2 Skin the peaches, remove the seeds and slice the fruit into the bowl. Cover the bowl and macerate for at least 1 hour in a cool place or the refrigerator.

3 Remove the cinnamon and cloves. Serve.

Serves 4-6

Cold Marbled Ricotta and Chocolate

125g (4oz) bitter chocolate, broken into small pieces

1 tspn softened butter

125g (4oz) sugar

60g (2oz) ricotta cheese

1 tblspn Cointreau

1 tspn almond essence

1 Combine the chocolate and butter in a heatproof bowl set over barely simmering water. Stir until completely melted and smooth. Remove from the heat and cool to room temperature.

2 Combine the sugar, ricotta, Cointreau and almond essence in a blender or food processor. Purée until smooth. Scrape into a serving bowl.

3 Pour the cooled chocolate over the ricotta mixture. Blend in with a skewer or spoon until an attractive, marbled effect has been achieved. Do not over-mix or the effect will be lost. Cover and chill for at least 6 hours before serving.

Serves 8-10

Pears with Ricotta and Walnuts

The pears for this dessert should be perfectly ripe but still relatively firm. Avoid any fruit which is bruised.

375g (12oz) ricotta cheese

60ml (2fl oz) double cream

60ml (2fl oz) nut-flavoured liqueur, optional

4 tblspn chopped fresh mint

6 dessert pears, peeled, halved and cored

12 walnut halves, roughly chopped

mint sprigs for garnish

1 In a bowl, combine the cheese and liqueur, if using. Add the chopped mint and beat the mixture until smooth.

2 Arrange the pears on 6 dessert plates. Top each with a few tablespoons of the cheese mixture, sprinkle with the walnuts, garnish with mint sprigs and serve.

Serves 6

Orange Cream Cheese Filled Figs

8 glace figs

Filling

155g (5oz) cream cheese, softened

2 tspn grated orange rind

2 tblspn orange-flavoured liqueur

30g (1oz) icing sugar, sifted

Syrup

125ml (4fl oz) freshly squeezed orange juice

1 tblspn lemon juice

2 tblspn sugar

1 To make the filling, beat the cream cheese with the orange rind, liqueur and icing sugar until creamy. Spoon 2 tablespoons of the filling into each glace fig, arrange 2 filled figs on each of 4 dessert plates, cover and chill.

2 Meanwhile make the syrup. Combine the orange juice, lemon juice and sugar in a small heavy-based saucepan over low heat. Bring slowly to the boil, then simmer for 5 minutes. Set aside to cool for 15 minutes; serve with the figs.

Serves 4

Variation

The filling is equally delicious served in fresh peach halves.

Orange Cream Cheese Filled Figs

French Apple Tarts

1 sheet ready-rolled puff pastry, thawed

egg yolk for glazing

2 Granny Smith apples, peeled, cored and very finely sliced

1 tblspn clear honey

1 tblspn caster sugar

whipped cream for serving

1 Preheat oven to 190°C (375°F/Gas 5). Cut pastry sheet into 4 squares. Cut a 5mm (1/4in) strip from each side of each square. Brush squares with egg yolk. Place pastry strips on top of each square around edges to form square pastry cases.

2 Brush each pastry case with egg yolk, place on dampened baking sheets and bake for 10 minutes.

3 Arrange apple slices in centre of each pastry case, brush with honey and sprinkle with sugar.

4 Bake for 15 minutes. Serve immediately, with whipped cream.
Serves 4

Grape Tart

500g (1lb) red grapes, halved

125ml (4fl oz) quince jelly

1 tblspn orange-flavoured liqueur

Hazelnut Pastry

185g (6oz) plain flour

pinch salt

75g (2 1/2 oz) ground hazelnuts

90g (3oz) butter, cubed

60g (2oz) caster sugar

2 egg yolks

iced water

1 Make hazelnut pastry. Combine flour, salt and hazelnuts in a large mixing bowl. Rub in butter until the mixture resembles coarse breadcrumbs. Add sugar, then stir in egg yolks with enough iced water to make a soft dough. Knead dough briefly on a lightly floured surface, wrap in greaseproof paper and refrigerate for 30 minutes.

2 Place pastry in middle of a 20cm (8in) loose-based tart tin. Using your fingers, press pastry out from middle towards edges to fill tin, making a pie shell that is slightly thicker on the sides than the base. Place in refrigerator for 1 hour, or in the freezer for 30 minutes.

3 Preheat oven to 180°C (350°F/Gas 4). Line pastry with foil, add baking beans and bake for 10 minutes. Remove foil and beans and bake for 20 minutes or until pastry is pale and firm. Remove to a wire rack to cool in tin; when cool, remove ring and base of tin.

4 Fill pastry case with grapes, cut sides down, making two layers. Melt jelly in a small saucepan over very low heat, stir in liqueur, pour over grapes and leave to set. Refrigerate for at least 1 hour before serving.
Serves 6

Kitchen Tip
The pastry can be made in a food processor. Combine all the ingredients except the iced water, pulse until mixture resembles coarse breadcrumbs, then, with the motor running, add iced water until the dough forms a ball.

Rich Chocolate Almond Dessert Cake

6 eggs, separated

185g (6oz) caster sugar

2 tblspn cocoa

100g (3 1/2 oz) ground almonds

100g (3 1/2 oz) dark chocolate, melted

icing sugar to decorate

1 Preheat oven to 180°C (350°F/Gas 4). Beat egg yolks and sugar in a large bowl until creamy. Beat in cocoa, almonds and chocolate; the mixture will be very thick.

2 In a separate bowl, beat egg whites until fluffy. Fold into chocolate mixture.

3 Pour mixture into a lined and greased 20cm (8in) round cake tin. Bake for 35-40 minutes.

4 Remove cake from oven and allow to cool in tin for 10 minutes. Transfer to a serving dish, dust with sifted icing sugar and serve.
Serves 8

French Apple Tarts

Plum and Apricot Clafouti

- 30g (1oz) self-raising flour
- 45g (1 1/2oz) plain flour
- 1 tspn caster sugar
- 90g (3oz) ground almonds
- 2 eggs
- 60g (2oz) butter, melted
- 150ml (5fl oz) milk
- 2 tblspn icing sugar
- 6 plums, stoned and roughly chopped
- 6 apricots, stoned and roughly chopped
- extra icing sugar for dusting

1 Preheat oven to 180°C (350°F/Gas 4). Sift flours into a medium bowl, stir in sugar and almonds and make a well in the centre. Mix eggs, butter and milk in a jug, pour into well and gradually incorporate flour to make a smooth batter.

2 Lightly grease a 23cm (9in) flan dish; sprinkle with icing sugar, shaking off excess. Spread plum and apricot pieces evenly over base of dish.

3 Pour batter over. Bake for 25-30 minutes. Dust with icing sugar.
Serves 6

Plum and Apricot Clafouti

Fresh Fig Fritters

- 6 fresh figs, peeled and quartered
- 125ml (4fl oz) brandy
- 2 tblspn sugar
- oil for deep frying

Batter

- 125g (4oz) plain flour
- 15g (1/2oz) butter, melted
- 75ml (2 1/2fl oz) beer
- 125ml (4fl oz) water
- 1 small egg
- 2 tspn brandy
- salt

1 Make batter by combining ingredients in a blender or food processor. Process until mixture is smooth. Set aside in a warm place for 1 hour.

2 Place figs in a heatproof dish. Combine brandy and sugar in a small saucepan. Bring to the boil, pour over figs and set aside for 30 minutes.

3 Drain figs; dry on paper towels. Whisk batter. Heat oil for deep frying.

4 Dip figs in batter and deep fry, a few at a time, until golden. Drain and serve.
Serves 6

Zabaglione

- 6 egg yolks
- 2 tblspn caster sugar
- 3 tblspn Marsala
- 1 tblspn finely grated orange rind

1 Beat egg yolks and sugar in top of a double boiler over simmering water until thick and pale.

2 Add Marsala and orange rind. Continue cooking, whisking constantly, until mixture thickens enough to coat the back of a spoon. Serve at once in dessert glasses.
Serves 4

Chocolate Tiramisu

- 2 eggs, separated
- 125g (4oz) caster sugar
- 375g (12oz) mascarpone
- 60ml (2fl oz) brandy
- pinch salt
- 200g (6 1/2oz) sponge fingers
- 60ml (2fl oz) strong black coffee, at room temperature
- sifted cocoa for dusting

1 In a bowl, beat egg yolks with sugar until mixture is pale and thick. Add mascarpone and brandy and beat until smooth.

2 In a separate bowl, beat egg whites with salt to soft peaks; fold into mascarpone mixture.

3 Arrange half the sponge fingers over base of a clear bowl. Sprinkle half the coffee over sponge fingers, then spread half mascarpone mixture on top. Repeat with remaining biscuits, coffee and mascarpone mixture. Dust top with sifted cocoa. Serve chilled.
Serves 8

Ricotta Custard

4 sponge fingers

2 tblspn Amaretto or other almond-flavoured liqueur

4 eggs

125g (4oz) caster sugar

200g (6½oz) ricotta cheese

2 tspn vanilla essence

30g (1oz) icing sugar

1 Place a sponge finger in each serving glass. Drizzle with liqueur and set aside.

2 In a bowl, beat eggs with caster sugar until light and fluffy. Combine ricotta, vanilla essence and icing sugar in a blender or food processor. Process until smooth. Scrape into bowl containing beaten eggs; beat until well combined.

3 Divide the mixture between the serving glasses. Chill for 30 minutes before serving.

Serves 4

Fresh Orange Jelly

6 oranges

1 lemon

75ml (2½fl oz) medium sherry

15g (½oz) leaf gelatine

60g (2oz) sugar

150ml (5fl oz) boiling water

1 Peel and segment 2 of the oranges; set the segments aside for decoration.

2 Peel remaining oranges and lemon very thinly, avoiding pith; soak peel in a bowl with sherry for 1 hour.

3 Combine gelatine and sugar in a medium bowl, add boiling water and stir until both gelatine and sugar have dissolved.

4 Strain sherry into bowl, discarding citrus rind. Squeeze juice from oranges and lemon; remove any pips but do not strain. Add juice to sherry mixture. Pour into a mould, rinsed with cold water. Refrigerate until set.

5 When ready to serve, unmould the jelly onto a large platter. Surround with the reserved orange segments.

Serves 4

Ricotta Hearts with Redcurrant Coulis

75g (2½oz) cream cheese

125ml (4fl oz) natural low fat yogurt

250g (8oz) ricotta cheese

2 tspn vanilla essence

2 egg whites

30g (1oz) icing sugar

315g (10oz) redcurrants or raspberries

60g (2oz) caster sugar

60ml (2fl oz) water

1 Combine the cream cheese, yogurt, ricotta and vanilla essence in a blender or food processor. Process until smooth.

2 In a bowl, beat the egg whites until fluffy, then gradually beat in the icing sugar until the mixture is thick and glossy. Fold the egg mixture into the cheese mixture, mixing lightly but thoroughly.

3 Lightly grease four 125ml (4fl oz) heart-shaped moulds. Carefully line with damp muslin. Spoon in the mixture, taking care to fill all corners. Place on a baking sheet and refrigerate for 4 hours until set.

4 To make the coulis, combine the redcurrants or raspberries, caster sugar and measured water in a small saucepan. Bring to the boil, then simmer for 3 minutes. Push the mixture through a sieve into a small bowl. Cool, then chill until required.

5 Unmould the ricotta hearts onto a serving dish, removing the muslin. Pour a little coulis over each mould. Serve.

Serves 4

Baklava

125g (4oz) butter

90g (3oz) sugar

150ml (¼pt) water

155g (5oz) walnuts, chopped

155g (5oz) blanched almonds, chopped

¼ tspn ground cinnamon

1 x 275g (9oz) packet filo pastry (12 sheets)

Syrup

220g (7oz) sugar

150ml (5fl oz) water

2 tblspn lemon juice

1 Preheat oven to 180°C (350°F/Gas 4). Melt 60g (2oz) of butter with sugar and water in a medium saucepan. Stir in walnuts and almonds. Mix well, add cinnamon and set aside.

2 Melt rest of butter; use some of it to grease a 28 x 18cm (11 x 7in) baking tin. Line tin with 4 sheets of filo, brushing each sheet with melted butter.

3 Spread half nut filling over filo and cover with 4 more sheets, again brushing each with melted butter. Cover with rest of nut mixture, then add 4 more sheets of filo, brushing each with butter as before. Brush butter over surface.

4 Using a sharp knife, cut surface layers of pie in diamond shapes. Bake for 40 minutes.

5 Meanwhile make syrup by mixing all ingredients in a small saucepan. Bring to boil and boil gently for 6 minutes. Cool slightly.

6 Pour syrup over baked baklava as soon as it is removed from oven. Set aside to cool. Allow to stand for 2-3 hours before serving, but do not chill.

Serves 10

Variation

Use 315g (10oz) chopped walnuts; omit the almonds. Add 4 tblspn clear honey to the syrup and increase the quantity of lemon juice to 3 tblspn.

Ricotta Custard

Mediterranean Food on the Menu

Mix and match menus from this collection of recipes

Italian Dinner for 4
Conjure up images of the sunny south with these Italian specialities.

Cherry Tomatoes with Parmesan and Rosemary
(page 6)

Veal Piccata
(page 24)

Wild Rice and Mushrooms
(page 22)

Buttered Beans and Pinenuts
(page 32)

Zabaglione
(page 41)

Vegetarian Choice
The Mediterranean region has much to offer the vegetarian, as this menu proves.

Polenta with Mushroom Sauce
(page 23)

Provençal Aubergines
(page 35)

Glazed Honey Onions
(page 32)

Broad Bean Salad
(page 36)

Fresh Fig Fritters
(page 41)

Pasta Party
Pasta is the perfect party choice: quick, easy and everybody's favourite.

Fettucine with Broad Beans, Red Peppers and Grainy Mustard
(page 20)

Spirelli with Tomato and Artichoke Sauce
(page 21)

Tagliatelle and Potatoes with Garlic and Oil
(page 20)

Italian Bean Salad
(page 6)

Radicchio and Pinenut Salad
(page 36)

Chocolate Tiramisu
(page 41)

Pears with Ricotta and Walnuts (page 38)

Spanish Celebration
Paella is such a substantial dish that it needs no starter. The orange jelly makes for a perfect ending.

Paella
(page 11)

Fresh Orange Jelly
(page 42)

Bouillabaisse

45

A Meal in Marseilles
A light salad refreshes the palate after this famous fish soup.

Bouillabaisse with rouille
(page 3)

Crusty bread

Endive and Mangetout Salad
(page 36)

Grilled Mustard Poussins
(page 31)

Pommes Patricia
(page 32)

Cheeses

Peaches in Wine
(page 38)

Marvellous Meze
You can make a meal of meze. Serve these tasty pastries and dips with plenty of pitta bread and dishes of black olives.

Greek Garlic Dip
(page 5)

Taramasalata
(page 5)

Tzatziki
(page 5)

Dolmades
(page 5)

Hummus
(page 7)

Borek
(page 7)

Pitta bread

Black olives

Sweet Pimiento Salad, Avgolemono

Provençal Lunch
All the warmth of the South of France is captured in this light summer menu.

Crudités with Aubergine and Olive Purée
(page 6)

Warm Mullet Niçoise
(page 12)

Potato and Courgette Bake
(page 33)

Ratatouille
(page 33)

Grape Tart in Hazelnut Crust
(page 40)

A Taste of the Islands
Greek dishes star on this after-theatre menu.

Avgolemono
(page 2)

Lemon and Lamb Kebabs with Yogurt
(page 26)

Greek Haricot Beans with Vegetables
(page 35)

Sweet Pimiento Salad
(page 36)

Baklava
(page 42) or fresh fruit

Useful Information

Length

Centimetres	Inches	Centimetres	Inches
0.5 (5mm)	1/4	18	7
1	1/2	20	8
2	3/4	23	9
2.5	1	25	10
4	1 1/2	30	12
5	2	35	14
6	2 1/2	40	16
7.5	3	45	18
10	4	50	20
15	6	NB: 1cm = 10 mm	

Metric/Imperial Conversion Chart

Mass (Weight)
(Approximate conversions for cookery purposes)

Metric	Imperial	Metric	Imperial
15g	1/2oz	315g	10oz
30g	1oz	350g	11oz
60g	2oz	375g	12oz (3/4lb)
90g	3oz	410g	13oz
125g	4oz (1/4lb)	440g	14oz
155g	5oz	470g	15oz
185g	6oz	500g (0.5kg)	16oz (1lb)
220g	7oz	750g	24oz (1 1/2lb)
250g	8oz (1/2lb)	1000g (1kg)	32oz (2lb)
280g	9oz	1500 (1.5kg)	3lb

Metric Spoon Sizes

1/4 teaspoon	= 1.25ml
1/2 teaspoon	= 2.5ml
1 teaspoon	= 5ml
1 tablespoon	=15ml

Liquids

Metric	Imperial
30ml	1fl oz
60 ml	2fl oz
90ml	3fl oz
125ml	4fl oz
155ml	5fl oz (1/4pt)
185ml	6fl oz
250ml	8fl oz
500ml	16fl oz
600ml	20fl oz (1pt)
750ml	1 1/4pt
1 litre	1 3/4pt
1.2 litres	2pt
1.5 litres	2 1/2pt
1.8 litres	3pt
2 litres	3 1/2pt
2.5 litres	4pt

Index

Avgolemono	2
Baklava	42
Beef with Sun-dried Tomatoes	24
Borek	7
Bouillabaisse	3
Bourride	12
Broad Bean Salad	36
Buttered Beans and Pinenuts	32
Calamari with Tomato Mint Sauce	12
Cherry Tomatoes with Parmesan and Rosemary	6
Chicken Marsala	31
Chicken, Tomato and Pimiento Casserole	31
Chocoate Tiramisu	41
Cold Marbled Ricotta and Chocolate	38
Crab Sauté with Prosciutto	9
Crudités with Aubergine and Olive Puree	6
Daube de Boeuf	29
Dolmades	5
Endive and Mangetout Salad	36
Fennel Salad	36
Fennel with Parmesan	32
Fettucine with Broad Beans, Red Peppers and Grainy Mustard	20
Fillet of Fish with Mustard Sauce	12
Fish Fillets with Prosciutto and Sun-dried Tomato Topping	11
French Apple Tarts	40
Fresh Fig Fritters	41
Fresh Orange Jelly	42
Fried Halibut Steaks with Oregano	10
Glazed Honey Onions	32
Grape Tart	40
Greek Garlic Dip	5
Greek Haricot Beans with Vegetables	35
Grilled Aubergine with Mozzarella	6
Grilled Mustard Poussins	31
Hearty Bean and Vegetable Soup	3
Hummus	7
Italian Bean Salad	6
Lamb and Lemon Kebabs with Yogurt	26
Lamb Stew with Lemon Sauce	28
Moules au Gratin	10
Moussaka	26
Mussels in Garlic and Basil Tomato Sauce	9
Omelette Roll with Sautéed Vegetables	18
Orange Cream Cheese Filled Figs	38
Paella	11
Parmesan Frittata	19
Peaches in Wine	38
Pears with Ricotta and Walnuts	38
Pickled Octopus Salad	10
Plum and Apricot Clafouti	41
Polenta with Mushroom Sauce	23
Pommes Patricia	32
Pork and Herb Patties with Aubergine Sauce	27
Potato and Cheese Gnocchi	17
Potato and Courgette Bake	33
Prawns with Feta	12
Provençal Aubergines	35
Provençal Baked Eggs	18
Radicchio and Pinenut Salad	36
Ratatouille	33
Rich Chocolate Almond Dessert Cake	40
Ricotta and Hazelnut Stuffed Potatoes	33
Ricotta Balls	18
Ricotta Custard	42
Ricotta Hearts with Redcurrant Coulis	42
Risotto with Ham and Lemon	23
Salad Niçoise	36
Sardinian Fish Stew	15
Sausage and Pancetta Risotto	22
Scallops with Parsley and Wine Sauce	14
Seafood Salad	14
Spaghetti with Raw Tomatoes and Herbs	21
Spanish Omelette	17
Spinach and Cheese Pie	19
Spirelli with Tomato and Artichoke Sauce	20
Sweet Pimiento Salad	36
Tagliatelle and Potatoes with Garlic and Oil	21
Taramasalata	5
Tomato and Bocconcini Salad	7
Tuna Steaks with Yogurt Cucumber Sauce	11
Turkish Artichoke and Potato Casserole	35
Tzatziki	5
Veal and Cheese Bundles	27
Veal Piccata	24
Veal Rolls in Tomato Sauce	29
Veal with Mozzarella	27
Veal with Mushroom and Parmesan Cream Sauce	24
Warm Mullet Niçoise	12
Warm Steamed Mussels with Orange Segments	14
Wild Rice and Mushrooms	22
Yogurt Soup	2
Zabaglione	41

Editorial Coordination: Merehurst Limited
Cookery Editors: Jenni Fleetwood, Katie Swallow
Editorial Assistant: Sheridan Packer
Production Manager: Sheridan Carter
Layout and Finished Art: Stephen Joesph
Cover Photography: David Gill
Cover Design: Maggie Aldred

Published by J.B. Fairfax Press Pty Limited
80-82 McLachlan Avenue
Rushcutters Bay 2011
A.C.N. 003 738 430

Formatted by J.B. Fairfax Press Pty Limited
Printed by Toppan Printing Co, Singapore

© J.B. Fairfax Press Pty Limited, 1993
This book is copyright. No part may be reproduced or transmitted without the written permission of the publisher. Enquiries should be made in writing to the publisher.

JBFP 292 A/UK
Includes Index
ISBN 1 86343 116 0 (set)
ISBN 1 86343 131 4

Distribution and Sales Enquiries
Australia: J.B. Fairfax Press Pty Limited
Ph: (02) 361 6366 Fax: (02) 360 6262
United Kingdom: J.B. Fairfax Press Limited
Ph (0933) 402330 Fax (0933) 402234

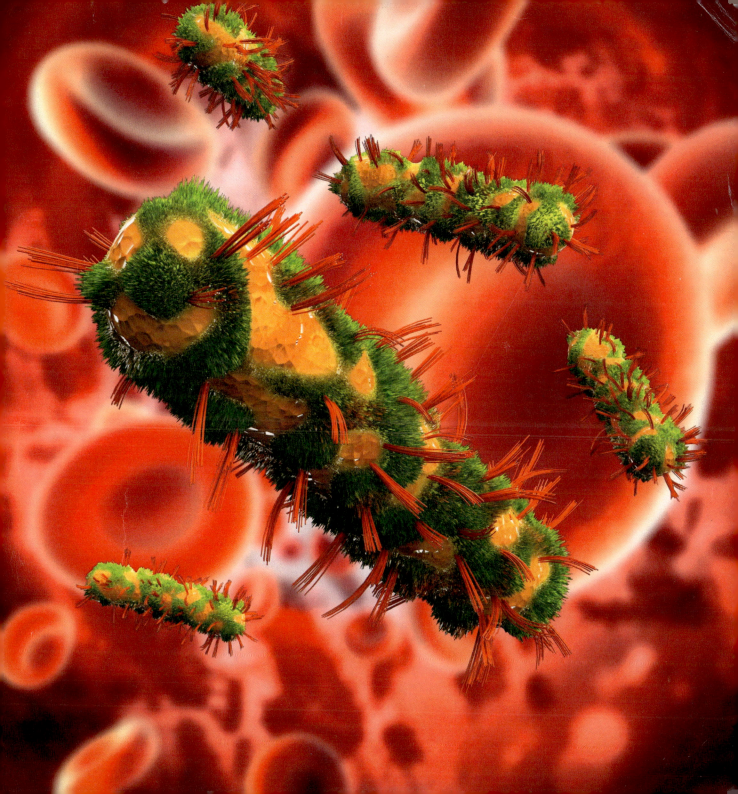

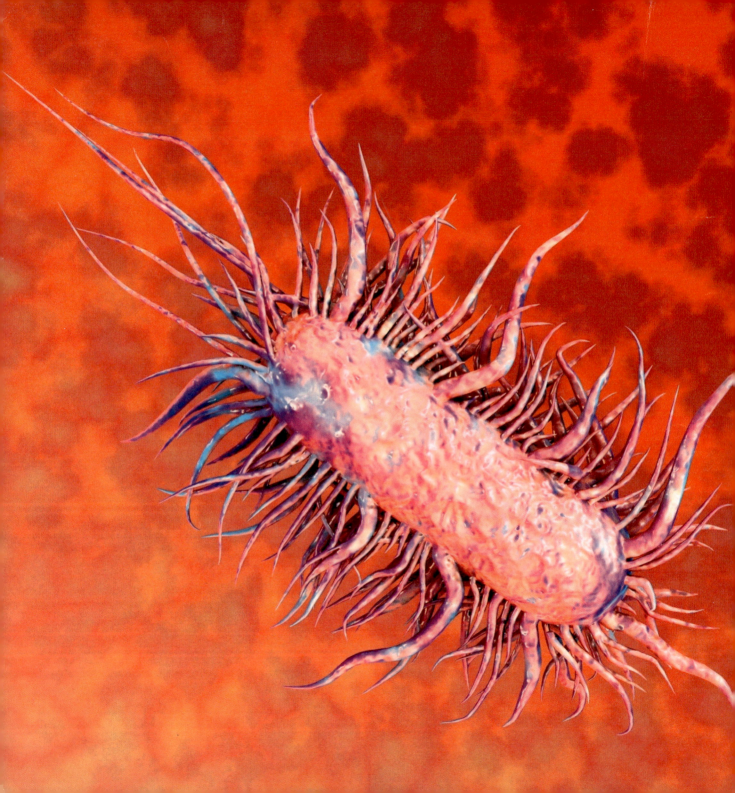

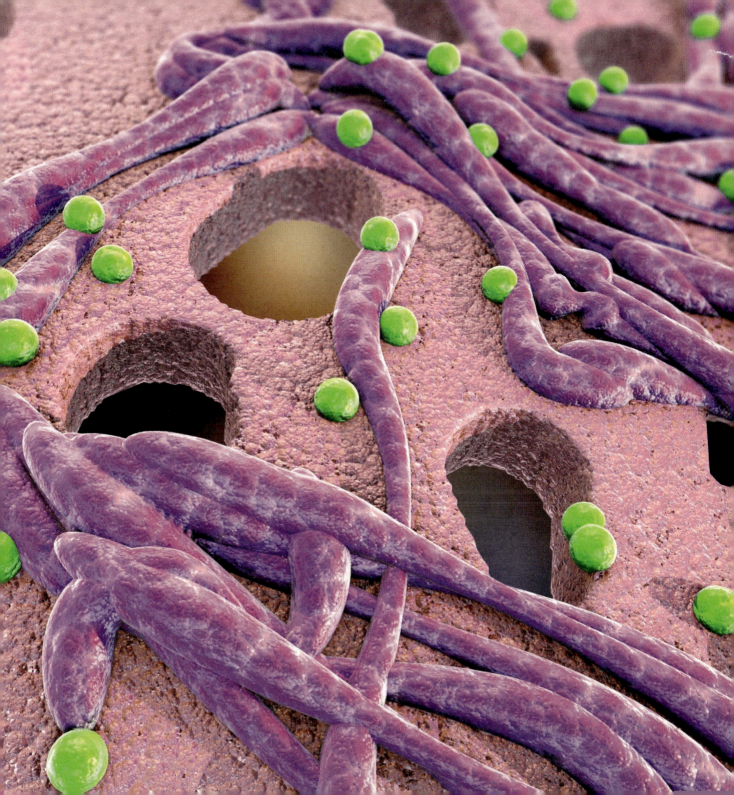

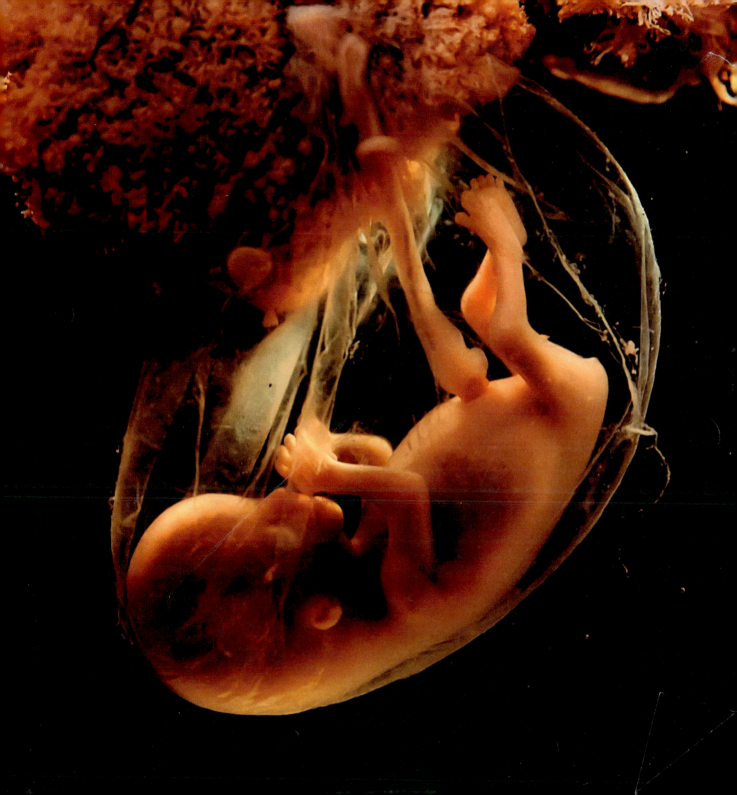

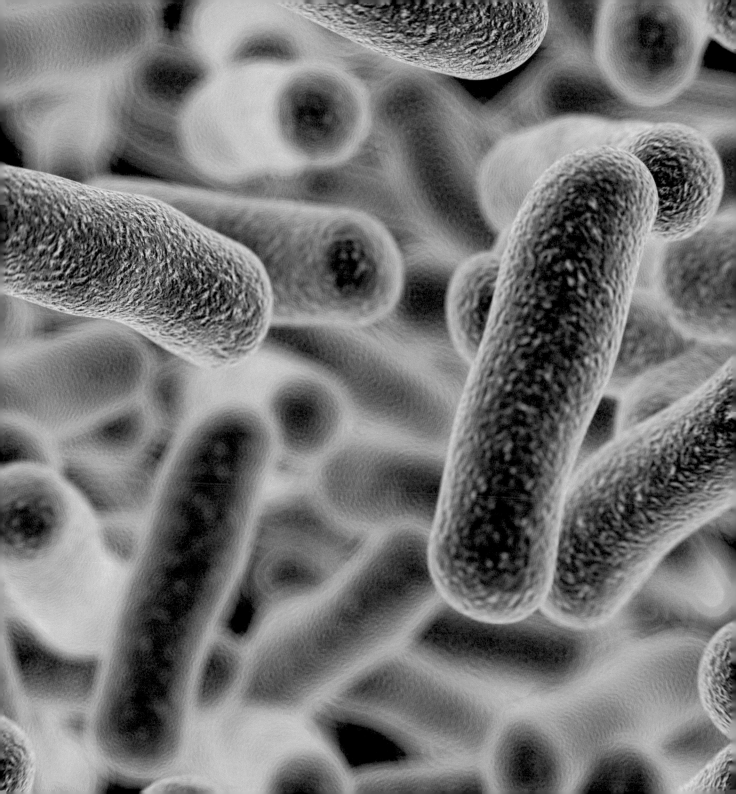

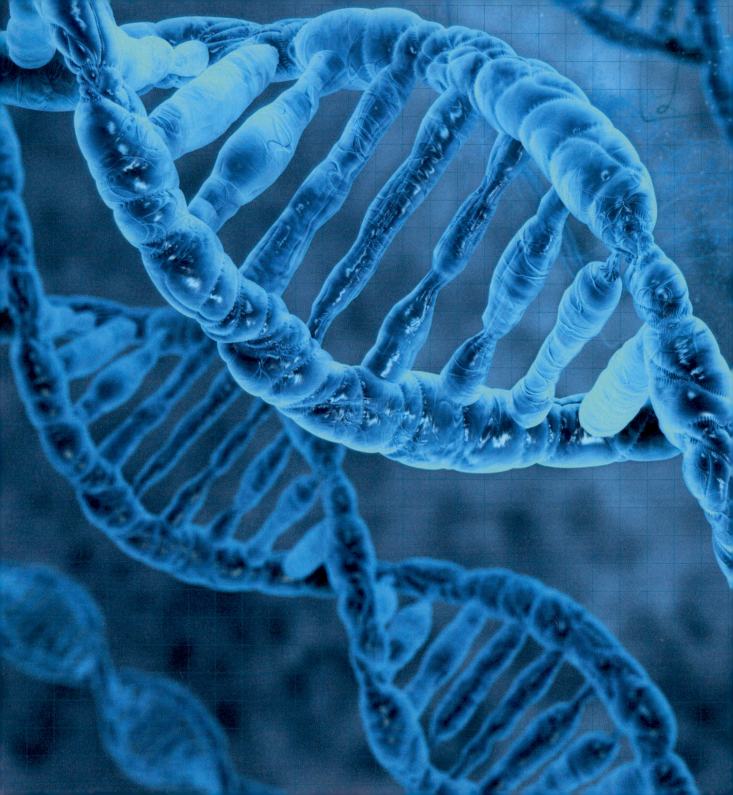

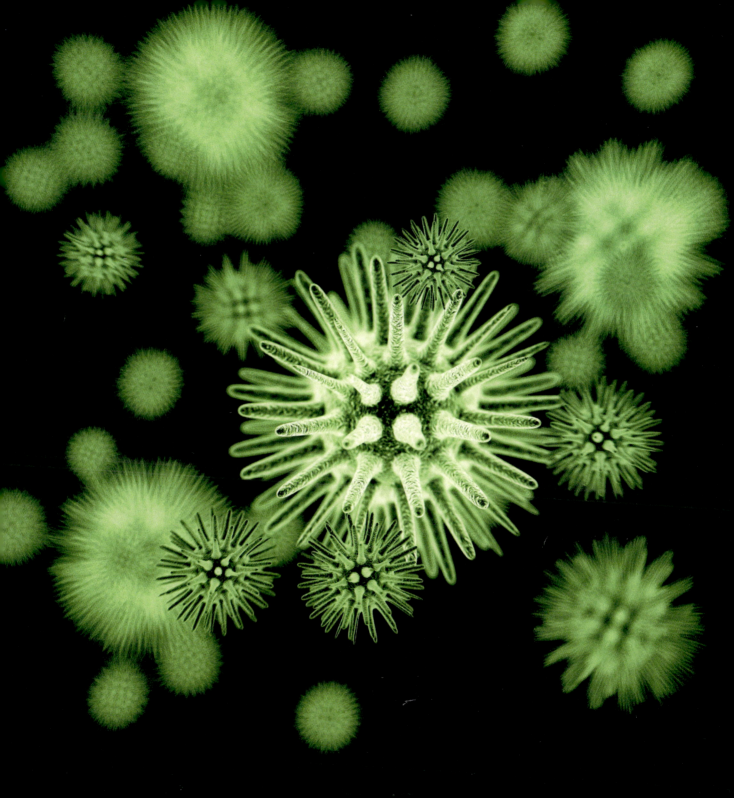

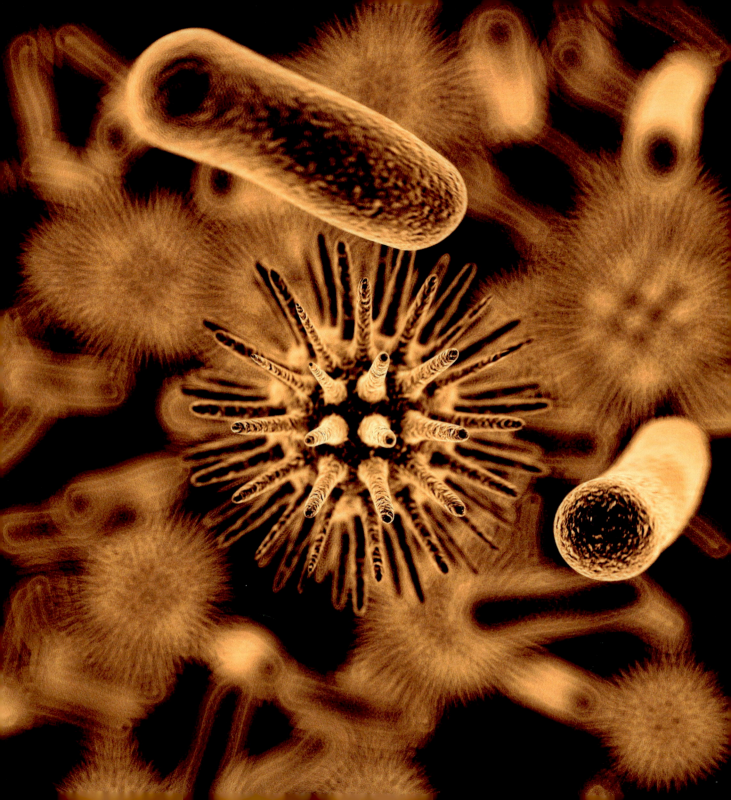

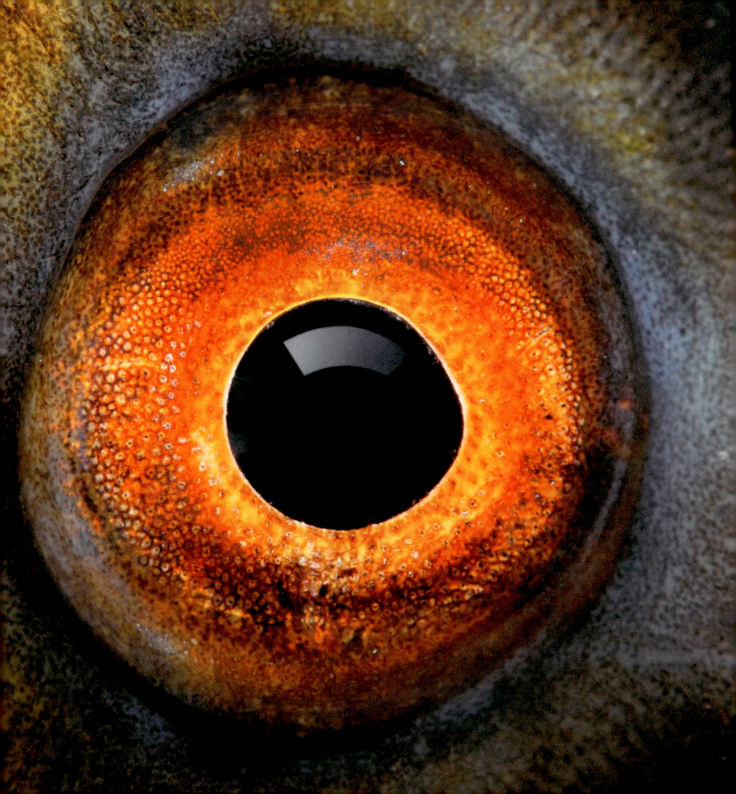

Made in the USA
Monee, IL
04 December 2019